War as Entertainment and Contents Tourism in Japan

This book examines the phenomenon of war-related contents tourism throughout Japanese history, from conflicts described in ancient Japanese myth through to contemporary depictions of fantasy and futuristic warfare.

It tackles two crucial questions: first, how does war transition from being traumatic to entertaining in the public imagination and works of popular culture; and second, how does visitation to war-related sites transition from being an act of mourning or commemorative pilgrimage to an act of devotion or fan pilgrimage? Representing the collaboration of ten expert researchers of Japanese popular culture and travel, it develops a theoretical framework for understanding war-related contents tourism and demonstrates the framework in practice via numerous short case studies across over a millennium of warfare in Japan including the tales of heroic deities in the *Kojiki* (Records of Ancient Matters, AD 712), the Edo poetry of Matsuo Basho, and the Pacific war through the lens of popular media such as the animated film *Grave of the Fireflies*.

This book will be of interest to researchers and students in tourism studies and cultural studies, as well as more general issues of war and peace in Japan, East Asia, and beyond.

Takayoshi Yamamura is a Professor at Hokkaido University, Japan.

Philip Seaton is a Professor at Tokyo University of Foreign Studies, Japan.

Routledge Focus on Asia

War as Entertainment and Contents Tourism in Japan

Edited by Takayoshi Yamamura and Philip Seaton

Routledge
Taylor & Francis Group

LONDON AND NEW YORK

First published 2022
by Routledge
4 Park Square, Milton Park, Abingdon, Oxon OX14 4RN

and by Routledge
605 Third Avenue, New York, NY 10158

Routledge is an imprint of the Taylor & Francis Group, an informa business

British Library Cataloguing-in-Publication Data
A catalogue record for this book is available from the British Library

Library of Congress Cataloging-in-Publication Data
Names: Seaton, Philip A., 1972- editor. | Yamamura, Takayoshi,
1971- editor.
Title: War as entertainment and contents tourism in Japan/edited by
Philip Seaton and Takayoshi Yamamura.
Identifiers: LCCN 2021061787 (print) | LCCN 2021061788 (ebook) |
ISBN 9781032145679 (hardback) | ISBN 9781032145693 (paperback) |
ISBN 9781003239970 (ebook)
Subjects: LCSH: Contents tourism–Japan. | Dark tourism–Japan. |
War and society–Japan.
Classification: LCC G156.5.C66 W37 2022 (print) | LCC G156.5.C66
(ebook) | DDC 306.4/819–dc23/eng20220218
LC record available at https://lccn.loc.gov/2021061787
LC ebook record available at https://lccn.loc.gov/2021061788

ISBN: 978-1-032-14567-9 (hbk)
ISBN: 978-1-032-14569-3 (pbk)
ISBN: 978-1-003-23997-0 (ebk)

DOI: 10.4324/9781003239970

Typeset in Bembo
by Deanta Global Publishing Services, Chennai, India

Contents

Figures

Contributors

Luli van der Does is an Associate Professor at Hiroshima University, Japan.

Yosuke Fujiki is a Professor at the University of Shiga Prefecture, Japan.

Kyungjae Jang is an Associate Professor at Hiroshima University, Japan.

Aleksandra Jaworowicz-Zimny is a Research and Teaching Assistant at Nicolaus Copernicus University, Poland.

Ryo Koarai is a PhD candidate at Hokkaido University, Japan.

Hitoshi Nakai is an Emeritus Professor at the University of Shiga Prefecture, Japan.

Philip Seaton is a Professor at Tokyo University of Foreign Studies, Japan.

Akiko Sugawa-Shimada is a Professor at Yokohama National University, Japan.

Qiaodan Wang is a PhD candidate at Tokyo University of Foreign Studies, Japan.

Takayoshi Yamamura is a Professor at Hokkaido University, Japan.

Preface

Philip Seaton

18 May 2019 – In front of a memorial stone, a middle-aged man clasps his hands in prayer and bows (Figure 0.1). It is a pose seen in Japan when people pause to remember and commemorate the dead. Just to his left is a young woman. She is dressed in the distinctive colours of Shinsengumi and has various Shinsengumi goods clearly visible in her bag. She holds up a stuffed toy and takes a picture in front of the memorial on her smartphone. Observing this scene is the author, who has travelled to Hakodate in the year of the 150th anniversary of the Battle of Hakodate (and the year before the COVID-19 pandemic laid savage waste to the Japanese tourism industry) to attend one of the city's main tourism events, the Goryōkaku Festival. I quickly take this photograph because this moment perfectly encapsulates the phenomenon I have come to observe and the topic of this book: *war-related contents tourism*.

The memorial stone is at the site of the Ippongi Gate, where Hijikata Toshizō, the feared vice-commander of Shinsengumi, is believed to have died during the Battle of Hakodate at the end of the Boshin War (1868–1869). It is a site of death in battle, and people have gathered here as part of a festival that keeps alive memories of the people who died (Chapter 10). People like the middle-aged man are commemorating, but not grieving. He is wearing smart casual clothes, and not formal mourning attire. Too much time has passed for anyone to feel close personal connections to those who died in 1869. After his act of commemoration, he returns to tourism/leisure mode – smiling and chatting in the warm spring sunshine with his companions. Meanwhile, there are a number of other people cosplaying as Shinsengumi members like the young woman. Their appearances and behaviours are characteristic of pop culture fans. Some have probably travelled long distances to be here. A few hours after taking the photo (Figure 0.1), I attended the competition to recreate Hijikata's death held at Goryōkaku Tower. A number of the competitors, like me, had travelled around 700 kilometres from Tokyo to be here.

Figure 0.1 At the site of Hijikata Toshizō's death. Author's photo.

Seven months later – In January 2020, I travelled to Hiroshima to visit the newly renovated Hiroshima Peace Memorial Museum. This was to be my last on-site observation of war-related tourism before the COVID-19 pandemic struck. Hiroshima is also a site of death in war. At the Cenotaph in the Peace Memorial Park, again people paused, clasped their hands together in prayer, and bowed in memory of those who perished. However, there were no cosplayers engaging in fan behaviours. Most people were in a similar contemplative mode to the middle-aged man I saw in Hakodate. But after their moment of commemoration, most visitors here too returned to smiling and talking to their travel companions on their visit to the Peace Memorial Park.

What connects Hakodate and Hiroshima is that – and forgive the intentionally jarring wording – war is a lucrative tourism resource for both cities. The Goryōkaku Festival is one of the flagship events of the Hakodate tourism calendar. Goryōkaku Fort is famous as the site of the last battle of the Boshin War. And the famous night view from the top of Mt Hakodate could be developed more easily for tourism in the postwar (the cable car opened in 1958) because in the prewar the Japanese military opened up access to the mountain top to position a gun battery there, protecting the Tsugaru Straits between southern Hokkaido and northern Honshu (the gun battery remains are a short hike from the cable car station). In Hiroshima, meanwhile, the city's 2019 tourism report lists the Hiroshima Peace Memorial Museum as the city's number two attraction, with 1.53 million visitors in 2018 (the Marina Hop Aquarium came top with 2.1 million visitors). Hiroshima Castle, which was destroyed during the bombing but rebuilt in 1958, attracted 304,908 visitors (Hiroshima City 2019). Hiroshima city would have been largely non-descript as a tourism destination for international visitors today without the A-bomb – except as a base for day trips to the UNESCO World Heritage Site of Itsukushima Shrine with its famous floating torii.

Where Hakodate and Hiroshima differ substantially, however, is in the uses to which the cities' war histories may be put as tourism resources. As already mentioned, in Hakodate there is a contest to reenact the death of Hijikata Toshizō. Could there ever be a contest to reenact the death of Sadako, the little girl who died of leukaemia after being exposed to radiation and whose story became famous because she folded a thousand origami cranes in the belief it would help her to recover? Would people go to the Cenotaph in Hiroshima in cosplay and take selfies to share on social media? Is it possible to be a 'fan of Hiroshima' by watching dramas and playing computer games in the same manner as many people become 'fans of Shinsengumi'? There are clearly major differences between the 'narrative qualities' (see Chapter 1) of war and death that history has bequeathed to the Hakodate and Hiroshima tourism industries. Ultimately, the aim of this book is to answer two questions: *first, how does war transition from being traumatic to entertaining in the public imagination and works of popular culture; and second, how does visitation to war-related sites transition from being an act of mourning or commemorative pilgrimage into an act of devotion or fan pilgrimage?*

There are many factors involved. The Boshin War is two generations further into the past than the Second World War. One was a civil war and one a global conflict. The memorial in Hakodate is for one soldier who chose to die a samurai's death for the cause to which he devoted his life. The Cenotaph in Hiroshima is for tens of thousands of civilians whose lives were extinguished one August morning. Not all wars are equal, and not all war deaths are equal. Accordingly, not all wars and deaths can be treated the same way within popular culture, heritage sites, and tourist attractions.

Japan is a particularly interesting case study in this regard as it has two marked yet contrasting approaches to the commodification of war in popular culture and tourism. The first is evident in Hakodate. Japan has a proud warrior tradition developed over centuries of samurai history. Popular culture depicting war as swashbuckling entertainment thrives on this history in the numerous period dramas, films, manga, anime, and computer games in samurai scenarios. The second is evident in Hiroshima. Having experienced heavy defeat, widespread destruction, and occupation within living memory, Japanese war memories of the Asia-Pacific War focus on the horrors of war. Japan has constructed a postwar image of a peace nation, exemplified in Article 9 of the Constitution, which states 'Japanese people forever renounce war as a sovereign right of the nation and the threat or use of force as means of settling international disputes'. War, therefore, has a fluid position within popular Japanese culture. It is both idealized and vilified, a source of entertainment and a subject of the utmost seriousness. This makes Japan an ideal case study for developing a theoretical framework about the connections between war, popular culture entertainment, and tourism.

About this book

In Chapter 1, Seaton and Yamamura outline a theoretical framework for war-related tourism and present the tourism policy context in Japan. The remaining sections then work chronologically through Japanese history. Part I (Chapters 2–5) goes up to the unification of Japan at the Battle of Sekigahara in 1600. Part II (Chapters 6–10) looks at the Edo period to the 1860s. Part III (Chapters 11–14) examines the Japanese Empire to the late 1920s. Part IV (Chapters 15–19) is about the Asia-Pacific War. And Part V (Chapters 20–23) considers war in the post-1945 era, from stories connected to the contemporary military (Japan Self-Defense Forces) through to fantasy/futuristic war. Finally, the conclusions draw together the main arguments and identify seven key patterns of war-related (contents) tourism.

As is customary in books about Japan, names are rendered in the Japanese order – family name followed by given name. Macrons indicate long vowel sounds but are omitted when there is a common English spelling without them, e.g. Tokyo.

Finally, the authors have prepared an online appendix to be used in conjunction with this open access publication. Much of the evidence for contents tourism exists online in the form of blogs, videos, tourism websites, and other such materials. Selected links relating to all the chapters may be accessed from:

Yamamura Takayoshi: https://yamamuratakayoshi.com/en/publica-tions-list/

Philip Seaton: https://philipseaton.net/research/books/

Access to all online resources in chapter reference lists was confirmed on 10 October 2021.

Reference

Hiroshima City, 2019. *Hiroshima-shi kankō jōkyō (heisei 30-nen, 2018 dētā)*. https://www.city.hiroshima.lg.jp/uploaded/attachment/107317.pdf.

Acknowledgements

This book presents research results from a three-year project (2019–2022) supported by the Japan Society for the Promotion of Science (grant number 19H04377, grant holder, Yamamura Takayoshi; research collaborators Philip Seaton, Sugawa Akiko, Fujiki Yosuke, Jang Kyungjae, and Luli van der Does). We express our sincere gratitude to JSPS for their financial support.

The chapter authors have received valuable information and materials from many people or institutions. Expressions of gratitude are made in individual chapters. We also thank all the support given by staff at Routledge throughout the whole process of taking this book to press. Whilst every care has been taken to ensure that no errors have been made in the book, any remaining errors are the responsibility of the chapter authors and editors.

Takayoshi Yamamura, Sapporo, November 2021

Periods of Japanese history

When periods or eras are mentioned in the text, they refer to the following year spans. The history of Japan comprises three concurrent histories that finally converge in 1869–1879:

1. The history of 'central Japan', namely Honshu (except for Tohoku), Shikoku, and northern Kyushu.
2. 'Northern history' (*hoppōshi*) centred on northern Honshu, Hokkaido (known before 1869 as Ezo by Japanese and as Yaunmosir by Ainu), and the Okhotsk Sea.
3. Ryukyu history (now Okinawa).

Jomon period (early hunter-gatherer period):	pre-ca. 300 BC
Mythical ascension of Emperor Jimmu:	660 BC
Yayoi period (introduction of rice culture):	ca. 300 BC–300 AD
Kofun period (burial mounds of kings):	250–538
Asuka period:	538–710
Nara period (capital in Nara):	710–794
Heian period (capital in Kyoto):	794–1185
War between the Mongol Empire and the Ainu:	1264–1308
Kamakura period (capital in Kamakura):	1185–1333
Kemmu restoration (overthrow of Kamakura government):	1333–1336
Ashikaga (Muromachi) period (government returns to Kyoto):	1336–1573
Northern and Southern Courts period (competing imperial courts):	1337–1392
Wajin (Japanese) presence established in Yaunmosir:	by the fifteenth century
Unification of the Ryukyu Kingdom (Shō Dynasty):	1429

xviii   *Periods of Japanese history*

Sengoku period (Warring States period):	1467–1590
Azuchi-Momoyama period (culmination of central Japan's unification):	1573–1603
Early Modern period (from Azuchi-Momoyama to Edo periods):	1573–1868
Edo period (period of the Tokugawa shogunate):	1603–1868
Matsumae clan trade monopoly in Ezo/Yaunmosir:	1604–1799, 1821–1855
Satsuma invasion of the Ryukyu Kingdom:	1609
Bakumatsu period (end of the shogunate):	1853–1868
Tokugawa shogunate direct rule of Ezo:	1799–1821, 1855–1869
Meiji period (reign of Emperor Meiji):	1868–1912
Annexation of Hokkaido:	1869
Annexation of Okinawa (Ryukyu Disposition):	1879
Taisho period (reign of Emperor Taisho):	1912–1926
Showa period (reign of Emperor Hirohito):	1926–1989
Postwar era:	1945–

1 Theorizing war-related contents tourism

Philip Seaton and Takayoshi Yamamura

The fundamental questions posed by this book are *first, how does war transition from being traumatic to entertaining in the public imagination and works of popular culture; and second, how does visitation to war-related sites transition from being an act of mourning or commemorative pilgrimage into an act of devotion or fan pilgrimage?* The transition between the immediate postwar situation and the time when war is extensively entertainmentized and touristified may be a bumpy, drawn-out process as a society negotiates within itself and with external others regarding the acceptable ways in which the wartime past may be represented, utilized, touristified, and travelled. Ultimately compromise emerges between what the moral/political milieu will allow and what the market for war representations and tourist sites will bear. This chapter presents a theoretical framework hypothesizing how these transformations occur. This then links to contemporary tourism policy in Japan and the ways in which Japan's municipalities have been encouraged by the central government to use local narratives (including local war narratives) as part of their regional revitalization and tourism promotion strategies.

From war memories to tourism imaginaries

The *war experiences* of soldiers and civilians are the raw materials of war discourses in a society. These experiences of war reach the ears of others via *composed narratives*. Oral historian Alistair Thomson (1994: 8) has identified 'composure' as:

> an aptly ambiguous term to describe the process of memory making. In one sense, we compose or construct memories using the public languages and meanings of our culture. In another sense we compose

DOI: 10.4324/9781003239970-1

memories that help us to feel relatively comfortable with our lives and identities, that give us a feeling of composure.

Composure of memories forms part of our (not necessarily successful) attempts to create a 'past we can live with' (ibid.: 9). Oral transmission creates shared memories and ultimately *collective memories* emerge within families, groups, and communities. Some narratives form the basis of *mediatized representations of war*, initially in news media but later in memoirs, novels, songs, and other works of popular culture. Other narratives are rooted in specific *sites of memory*, such as a battlefield or other sites of a significant wartime incident. These locations are initially marked simply – perhaps with a flag, bouquet of flowers, or grave marker – or become iconic place names or signifiers ('Hiroshima') via repeated media reportage. When sites of memory become sites of *commemorative pilgrimage*, there are the beginnings of a touristification process. The sites are developed over time and become popularized as sites of heritage tourism. Discourses regarding the meanings of these memories, narratives, mediatized representations, and tourist/heritage sites circulate within society. At close temporal proximity to the war, identification with war narratives rests heavily on political, national, and cultural identities, while emotional engagement is primarily via mourning, commemoration, or political/national belonging (Figure 1.1).

These processes at relatively close proximity to a war form the background context in which works of popular culture entertainment and war-related contents tourism ultimately emerge. Let us now fast forward by an unspecified amount of time – the exact amount depends on the circumstances. Now the raw materials are less the first-hand experiences of witnesses but rather the second-hand narratives of contemporary historians. *War history* – as told in non-fiction representations produced primarily by professional historians following codes of accuracy and objectivity – is utilized by various actors who edit, reference, and interpret history according to their needs. Over time, shared and collective memories of ordinary people have metamorphosed into *cultural memories* of war shared by members of a community. These communities are not just nations, ethnic groups, or cultures. Another form of cultural community is a fandom, and membership of war-related fandoms signifies a deep and active interest in a *narrative world* based on historical wars.

With the passage of time, mediatized representations of past wars reduce significantly within news and current affairs outlets and become predominately *works of war-related entertainment*. Individuals – as both

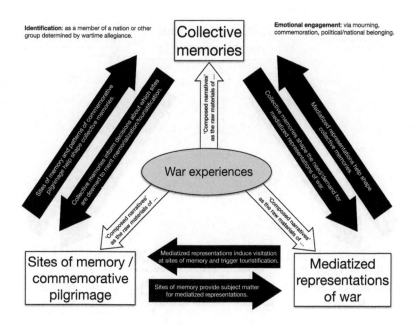

Figure 1.1 Societal discourses based on war experiences at relatively close temporal proximity to war. Prepared by the authors.

politically minded citizens and fans of historical entertainment – consume these works and travel to war-related sites. By this time, sites have undergone significant touristification, including the construction of museums, creation of war-related attractions, and provision of tourism products such as battlefield guided tours. Tourists exhibit motivations or behaviours that blend features of heritage tourism and contents tourism in a phenomenon we have labelled *heritage and/or contents tourism* (Seaton *et al.* 2017: 32–33). Once again, all narratives and activities circulating in a society continually reshape the nature of the war history being told. History is produced by people susceptible to the surrounding influences within the society in which they live, so even supposedly 'objective' history assumes some characteristics of cultural memories. Cultural activities may also unearth new evidence about the past, including new testimonies, hitherto unseen documents, and archaeological evidence. History itself, therefore, is constantly edited, interpreted, and rewritten with reference to the contemporary cultural milieu (Figure 1.2).

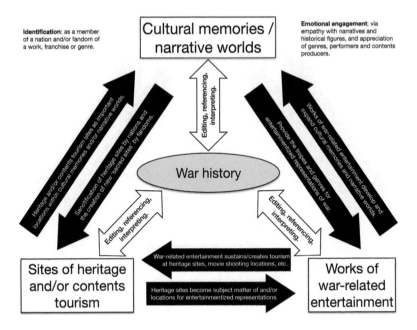

Figure 1.2 Societal discourses based on war history at a relatively far temporal distance from war. Prepared by the authors.

Imaginaries

From a tourism perspective, the net result of these processes within society is a set of three interconnecting *tourism imaginaries* (Figure 1.3), defined by Athinodoros Chronis (2012: 1797) as 'value-laden, emotion-conferring collective narrative constructions that are associated with and enacted in a particular place through tourism'.

The first is *imaginaries of (subjective) war experiences*. Here the focus is on 'our' history and 'our' cultural memories. Travel is essentially 'commemorative pilgrimage' that validates and reinforces our political and personal identities via travel to and embodied practice at sites related to past conflicts. Examples include visits to national monuments for largely ideological reasons, for example, visits to Yasukuni Shrine (Chapter 15).

The second is *imaginaries of (objective) war heritage*. War history is seen as the experience of 'others' (whether from another nation or another era). The history has objectified heritage value, perhaps enhanced by inclusion on (inter)national heritage lists like UNESCO World Heritage. Travel is essentially an 'educational rite of passage' to a place it is deemed important to visit for reasons of personal knowledge and growth. Consequently, the

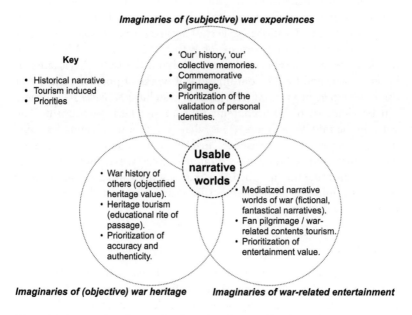

Figure 1.3 Imaginaries of war-related tourism. Prepared by the authors.

accuracy of information and authenticity of the experience gained is of high priority to visitors. Many visitors to such sites are international travellers. In Japan, the key example is Hiroshima, where people can stand at the very place ('site of memory') where the first atomic bomb was dropped in war and use the tourism experience to reflect upon global issues of war, peace, and (nuclear) disarmament.

The third is *imaginaries of war-related entertainment*. Wars are the subject of or backdrop to works of popular culture, whose appeal lies in their qualities as war-related entertainment. Travel to related sites is essentially 'fan pilgrimage' or war-related contents tourism. The narratives and characters possible in works of entertainment are limited only by the imaginations of creators and fans. War depictions range from semi-fictionalized to fantastical, while the levels of historical authenticity and accuracy required by fans in both works and tourist sites may fluctuate drastically from case to case. However, a common pattern within works of historical entertainment is that while great attention is paid to the 'look of the past' (Rosenstone 2000: 31) such as armour/weapon design or architectural styles, considerable liberties are taken with the flow of historical events.

These three imaginaries, whether singly or in combination, under-pin war-related tourism. A visit to a domestic war site might combine the political and educational aspects of an imaginary of (subjective) war experiences and an imaginary of (objective) war heritage. A visit to an overseas site, by contrast, might focus only on the latter. If visitation is heavily motivated by the consumption of works of popular culture (for example, a person visits Auschwitz after watching *Schindler's List*) there can be elements of both contents tourism and heritage tourism. The space in the middle of Figure 1.3 is where the tourism imaginaries combine to enable travel experiences that are simultaneously entertaining, educational, and self-affirming. War narratives where the imaginaries overlap constitute the most usable narrative worlds and generate many of the most significant and commercially viable war-related tourism phenomena in a society.

Authenticity

Using the notion of 'borders of memory', Edward Boyle (2019: 294) notes '[t]he differences between the collective memories of different groups means that … heritage sites become locations at which both the affirmation and contestation of collective memories occurs'. Such borders *within* sites can also exist among tourism actors. In sites of war-related tourism, misunderstandings and mutual distrust can occur between local communities and tourists, as well as between commemorative pilgrims, heritage tourists, and contents tourists. This is because the three imaginaries (Figure 1.3) constitute fundamentally different historical narratives, induce different forms of tourism, and are based on different values that should be prioritized. Furthermore, there can be multiple imaginaries within a single traveller, which can cause internal conflict and confusion in individuals while they are at war-related sites.

The concept of the 'interpretive community' (Fish 2004) elucidates this structure. In literary studies, 'interpretive communities' refer to 'groups of readers who share a set of conventions for understanding literary works in certain ways'. Furthermore, 'the formal properties of literary works exist only as they are activated by such communities of readers' and '[l]iterature, in other words, is both production and consumption at once' (Fish 2004: 217). Consequently, an interpretive community is a group that shares norms and codes for understanding and interpreting literary works. Figure 1.3 can be reinterpreted, therefore, as follows. Each of the three tourism imaginaries has a different set of conventions for understanding, encoding, and decoding war-related narratives. The interpretive communities sharing these norms are also different. Furthermore, fidelity to these norms and legitimacy in the process of interpretation are the criteria for authenticity in each community. Thus, there are at least three different standards of authenticity in the field of war-related tourism. As Gravari-Barbas and Graburn note, tourists 'decode the images of local authenticity based on imaginaries produced since the early days of tourism' (Gravari-Barbas and Graburn 2012: para.8).

When different tourism practices, such as heritage tourism and contents tourism, are developed in the same place, there are 'varying degrees of "authenticity"'. Objects, places, or practices authentic for contents tourists may be inauthentic for heritage tourists, and vice versa (Seaton *et al.* 2017: 31). The situation is even more complicated in transnational contents tourism phenomena. Accordingly, the challenge of tourism management at war-related sites is how the gulfs between different interpretations, norms, and standards of authenticity can be bridged, and how mutually acceptable and shareable narrative worlds can be created.

War/atrocity as entertainment and tourism resource

Given sufficient time, any war can be adapted for use in entertainment and/or tourism, although various factors affect the speed of this process. There is no magical formula determining this speed. However, the variables become evident by considering how war's 'least entertaining' aspects can be represented in works of entertainment that induce tourism.

Oda Nobunaga (1534–1582) was one of the three unifiers of Japan during the sixteenth century. Now he is one of Japan's most respected historical figures and is depicted in numerous dramas, anime, computer games, and tourist sites. However, he is also infamous for ordering merciless post-battle massacres in which tens of thousands of defeated samurai and ordinary civilians were slaughtered. Were he a modern-day figure, his position within Japanese pop culture and tourism would be deeply controversial. Yet over time, his victims' voices have disappeared into the void of unrecorded history, while his political achievements survive. Entertainmentization of Nobunaga is achieved via the selective remembering and representation of historical events. His cruelty is not denied but rather sanitized or marginalized.

Nobunaga's massacres, with sufficient passage of time, have not damaged his usability as a tourism resource. However, many will feel a certain resistance towards categorizing people who visit the Memorial Hall of the Victims in Nanjing Massacre by Japanese Invaders [sic.] after seeing a film like *City of Life and Death* as 'contents tourists'. The same can be said for those who visit Auschwitz after seeing *Schindler's List*, or Hiroshima after reading *Black Rain*. These examples feel fundamentally different to the prevalent image of contents tourism, such as anime pilgrimage or visits to Disneyland. Nevertheless, visiting harrowing war-related sites after consuming popular culture does meet our basic definition of contents tourism, namely 'travel behavior motivated fully or partially by narratives, characters, locations and other creative elements of popular culture forms' (Seaton *et al.* 2017: 3). However, the emphasis is on *partially* motivated. Sue Beeton (2015: 101), for example, recounts how viewing *The Killing Fields* influenced her decision to visit Cambodia and sites related to Khmer Rouge atrocities, although other factors (particularly her memories of a student from Cambodia) were also significant.

Travel to a harrowing war-related site is more likely to resemble a religious, educational, or commemorative pilgrimage than a fan pilgrimage. Unless, that is, the depiction of atrocity and suffering is sufficiently marginalized or in the background to allow the popular culture work to generate fans based on its more entertainment-focused narratives, characters, locations, and creative elements (a good example here is the anime *In This Corner of the World* – see Chapter 16). This is not to say that brutal depictions of wartime cruelty are unable to generate fandoms and contents tourism. *Game of Thrones* is notorious for its graphic violence and sexual content but has a loyal fandom that visits filming locations. In fantasy war scenarios far removed from our day-to-day lives – whether in a quasi-medieval era like *Game of Thrones* or a futuristic sci-fi tale – killing and abject cruelty can even be *the* fundamental ingredients of war-related entertainment.

The key to understanding the mainstream entertainmentization and 'contentsization' (Yamamura 2020) of war history – namely productions that achieve a basic level of commercial success and trigger identifiable levels of war-related contents tourism – is identifying how war history metamorphoses into a marketable *narrative* and how historical figures become fandom-generating *characters*. By becoming a marketable narrative, history assumes the characteristics of 'narrative worlds' (Seaton *et al.* 2017: 5) and induces tourism to 'places of the imagination' (Reijnders 2011: 14). Historical accuracy is not the issue. Rather the issue is how easily actual history can be shoe-horned into a tried and tested narrative format for entertainment storytelling, whether action-adventure, tragedy, human drama, or comedy. And authenticity in the tourism experience is not achieved via fidelity to the historical record but via the fidelity of the site's narrative/experience to the culture of the fandom or 'interpretative community'.

Regarding the creation of characters, there are two interlinked processes: hero creation and *kyarakutā* (character) creation. The former is not associated with a particular national context, but the latter has a Japanese nuance.

The main aspect of hero creation is defining the function that the character plays within the narrative. In the context of Japanese Asia-Pacific War cinema, Seaton has identified three types of heroes: military heroes, good Japanese, and victim-heroes (Seaton 2007: 152–3). A military hero is on a mission and overcomes various obstacles before succeeding, or failing nobly, in the end. This genre lends itself well to nationalistic storytelling and tourism at battlefields or war museums, for example, contents tourism relating to kamikaze pilots (Seaton 2019b). Victim-heroes, meanwhile, are characters whose suffering generates strong empathy among the audience. *Grave of the Fireflies* (Chapter 17) is a film in this genre that has triggered contents tourism. 'Good Japanese' are those who resist militaristic villains in narratives critical of Japan's wars and empire. These works are less likely to trigger contents tourism, but when they do there is a high heritage tourism component (cf. Sue Beeton's trip to Cambodia described above).

The main aspect of '*kyarakutā* creation' (*kyarakutā-ka*) is the representation of historical figures in an attractive style consistent with pop culture aesthetics developed in the worlds of manga and anime. Fans identify with a *kyarakutā* through visual, physical, or stylistic attraction as much as – or even more than – empathy with the figure's actual persona and/or role in history. For male figures, the archetype is the *ikemen* or heartthrob (Chapters 8, 10, and 14). For female characters, *moe* elements designed to be cute (*kawaii*) or sexually alluring to fans – for example, large manga-esque eyes or a girlish high-pitched voice – are used (Chapters 11, 14, and 20). Some historical figures have seen complete transformations in levels of fan interest as a result of stylized images that transform them into 'characters' – for example, Katakura Kojūrō (1557–1615) in the PlayStation game *Sengoku BASARA* (Seaton *et al* 2017: 86).

The process of crafting historical wars and figures into usable narratives and characters exists for any war in Japanese history. Generally speaking, events from a century ago have largely disappeared from living memory and can be entertainmentized with relatively little political fallout. The contrasting representations of the post-1950 Japan Self-Defense Force (Chapter 22) and pre-1945 Imperial Japanese Army in popular culture demonstrate that 'modern but less controversial' military narrative worlds are entertainmentized differently than 'earlier but more controversial' worlds. Furthermore, when contemporary political conflict has an intercultural dimension – particularly involving those groups on the receiving end of Japanese imperialism such as the Ainu (Hokkaido, Chapter 11), Ryukyuans (Okinawa, Chapter 6), Chinese, Taiwanese, and Koreans – pop culture representations and tourism can have international repercussions and/or feed into domestic war responsibility debates.

The cut-off point in Japan before which most narratives can be represented as historical entertainment largely free of contemporary political controversy is the 1870s. Domestic wars until the Satsuma Rebellion (1877) feature regularly in entertainment; characters from any side of these domestic wars (victors, losers, rulers, usurpers) are treated as heroes; and, war-related sites and events are treated as tourism resources by local authorities. However, controversial historical events with an international or intercultural dimension that generate Japan's 'history issue' (*rekishi mondai*) impinge on popular culture and tourism, starting with the annexation of Hokkaido after the Boshin War (1869). Later victorious wars (notably the Russo-Japanese War – Chapter 12) and victorious battles (such as Pearl Harbor) have featured in numerous military action-adventure works, mostly with a jingoistic tone. The expansionist wars of the 1930s and 1940s spawn diverse works from nationalistic action-adventure to self-critical human dramas to comedy. All can generate contents tourism, but in Japan, the productions featuring military heroes or victim-heroes are most likely to generate fandoms and travel behaviours commensurate with the common image of contents tourism as fan pilgrimage.

This idea of a cut-off point beyond which war/atrocity becomes usable in entertainment connects to a key debate within dark tourism studies, namely: Is there a point in history at which tourism connected to death, suffering, and the macabre (as is much war-related tourism) stops being 'dark tourism'? The role of media and the concept of 'chronological distance' in Lennon and Foley's original formulation of dark tourism (Lennon and Foley 2010: 11–12) create an important overlap with discussions of war-related contents tourism. In this context, Philip Seaton (2019a: 300) has proposed that war-related tourism emerges in four main phases:

1. Tourism during the war to warzones.
2. Immediate postwar tourism to sites of recent combat (before any widespread commercial touristification).
3. Commercial touristification of war-related sites and organized commemorative visitation.

4. Tourism to historical sites that remain relevant in the public imagination because works of popular culture generate new interest, forms of remembrance, and patterns of tourism.

Within this broad schema, not all wars or even events within a particular war go through these phases of touristification at the same speed. Subsequent wars can also reset the temporal context. Japan's early victories in the Manchurian Incident (1931) and China War (1937–1945) boosted tourism to China in the late 1930s (Kushner 2006: 45). The Japan Tourist Bureau (JTB) even opened an office in Nanjing in 1939, just over a year after the notorious massacre that occurred there (Ruoff 2014: 183). This jingoistic touristic demand collapsed, however, when the war turned against Japan after 1941. It also changed character completely after 1945. Following the normalization of relations with China in the 1970s, war-related tourism by the Japanese to Nanjing has often assumed the form of the 'apology and reconciliation tour'.

In places where local memories are of terrible suffering, host communities may resist the development of tourism. Gerald Figal describes the slow process by which postwar tourism in Okinawa developed out of commemorative tours by bereaved relatives to Battle of Okinawa sites. Okinawa's tourism image today as a tropical island paradise (Chapter 6) masks a tragic history, and for many years 'amusements on "sacred ground" in the southern part of Okinawa Island were considered in bad taste if not outright sacrilegious; establishing swimming beaches along the coast where the enemy had come ashore seemed out of place' (Figal 2012: 205). As in Nanjing or Hiroshima (Zwigenberg 2014), a site of mass death did not easily undergo touristification. Nevertheless, mass tourism ultimately emerged; and interest in Okinawa's war sites is now partially maintained by depictions of the Battle of Okinawa in films and dramas, such as the many renditions of the story of the Himeyuri 'Lily' Corps of schoolgirl nurses.

In short, there is no set pattern or timescale by which the entertainmentization and touristification of past wars proceed. In macro terms history loses its political sting the further it slips into the past. Positive conditions – such as victory in the war, a quickly-composed dominant narrative suited to entertainmentization, and postwar stability conducive to the rapid restart of entertainment production and tourism – enable swifter entertainmentization and touristification. By contrast, negative conditions – such as defeat, lingering recriminations over the war, and postwar instability – render these processes slower (Figure 1.4).

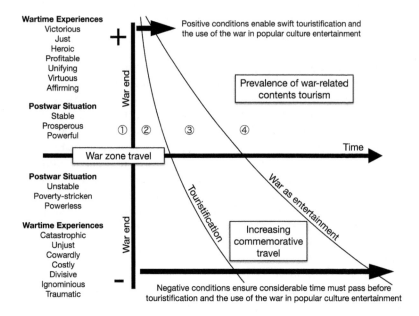

Figure 1.4 Four phases in the emergence of war-related contents tourism. Prepared by the authors.

Contents tourism policy and the use of history and stories

In this final section, we focus on how the emergence of war-related entertainment and tourism connects to Japanese government tourism policy in the 2000s (Yamamura and Seaton 2020). Japan's contents tourism policy began in earnest in 2005, when a report first defined contents tourism as 'tourism that utilizes media content related to a local area (films, TV dramas, novels, comic books, games, *etc.*) to promote tourism activities and related industries', and stated that 'the heart of contents tourism is to add "narrative quality" and "thematic quality" as a local atmosphere or image fostered through media contents' and 'to utilize narrative quality as a tourism resource' (Ministry of Land, Infrastructure & Transport *et al.*, 2005: 49). The 2005 report is largely devoid of perspectives on access to, protection of, and transmission of history and folklore. It only states that film commissions should 'effectively provide local information (events, local products, history, scenery, *etc.*)' to attract filmmakers (Ministry of Land, Infrastructure & Transport *et al.*, 2005:

21). Contents tourism policy, therefore, was not initially related directly to the preservation, transmission, or use of local history or local stories. The connections between war-related tourism and contents tourism were tenuous unless newly created narrative worlds depicted fictionalized or semi-fictionalized war.

In 2010, the Ministry of Economy, Trade and Industry (METI) established the Cool Japan Promotion Office, thereby initiating the Cool Japan policy. It was first launched as an economic policy promoting the export of goods and services incorporating characteristics of Japanese lifestyle and culture (both popular and traditional) that foreigners considered 'cool'. Then in 2011, the Intellectual Property Strategy Headquarters, established by the cabinet, announced its *Action plan on Cool Japan promotion*, elevating the Cool Japan strategy beyond mere economic policy. The plan aimed to promote the Cool Japan strategy on a cross-ministerial basis, with the cabinet taking the initiative. It included the promotion of tourism and regional revitalization through the use of cultural heritage by the Ministry of Education, Culture, Sports, Science and Technology, and the dissemination of tourism information related to cultural heritage by the Ministry of Land, Infrastructure, Transport and Tourism (Intellectual Property Strategy Headquarters 2011: 16). This facilitated the incorporation of cultural heritage into the Cool Japan strategy, and thus a link between popular culture content and cultural heritage was created within Japanese government policy. This was an important turning point.

In 2013, the Japan Tourism Agency (JTA), Japan National Tourism Organization (JNTO), METI, and Japan External Trade Organization (JETRO) collectively announced the *Joint action plan for increasing foreign visitors to Japan*, which emphasized that contents tourism was an important component of the Cool Japan policy framework. It was explicitly stated that as a result of exporting Japanese content and creating a Japan boom in other countries, the policy would 'encourage people to visit tourist destinations (headquarters or sacred places) that are recalled from Cool Japan content' (Japan Tourism Agency *et al.* 2013: 2). In this way, contents tourism policy was promoted as part of the Cool Japan strategy. Links between contents tourism policy and cultural heritage conservation policy then began to emerge. The Cool Japan strategy has become a full-fledged national policy, and both tourism and cultural heritage conservation and utilization have been incorporated within that strategy.

The Agency for Cultural Affairs, which is in charge of cultural heritage conservation and utilization, has established a project called 'Japan

Heritage'. It started accepting applications for the first phase in 2015. The purpose of this system is as follows:

> Japan's tangible and intangible cultural properties have been pre-served *through narratives* based on unique regional histories and tra-ditions. By recognizing these *stories* as Japan Heritage, the Agency plans to promote these historical legacies and to provide compre-hensive support so that this heritage may be effectively preserved and maintained.
>
> (Agency for Cultural Affairs n.d.: 1; emphasis added)

The Agency alludes to a shift from the traditional approach of conserva-tion-oriented management and administration of cultural properties to a utilization-oriented approach of promoting packaged cultural properties both domestically and internationally, based on the concept of recogniz-ing 'the narratives that bind Japan's regional cultural properties' (Agency for Cultural Affairs n.d.: 1) (Figure 1.5). As a result of this policy shift, the approach regarding contents tourism, in which a narrative is given to the region and tourists consume that narrative, is mirrored in the field of cultural heritage conservation. As indicated in Figure 1.5 by the inclusion of 'ancient armor' and 'castle', many of the important stories linked to such sites are war related.

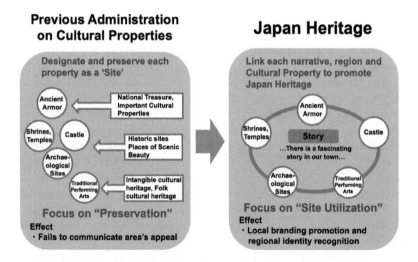

Figure 1.5 Primary objectives of 'Japan Heritage'. Prepared by the authors based on Agency for Cultural Affairs (n.d.: 1).

Heritage within the Cool Japan strategy

In June 2018, the Intellectual Property Strategy Headquarters released the *Intellectual property strategy vision*, which acknowledges the Cool Japan policy as part of the Japanese government's intellectual property strategy. In September 2019, they released the *Cool Japan strategy*, which included the following noteworthy statements:

> The use of stories/narratives has a variety of advantages that go beyond the effective promotion of attractions. Creating a story/narrative based on Japanese history, traditions, or culture is an opportunity to learn about Japanese history, *etc.*, and to (re)discover the essence of Japan, including its attractions and their backgrounds, which can lead to the development of human resources. The various elements included in the story/narrative can serve as a catalyst for collaboration across industries and regions, leading to the creation of new value.
>
> (Intellectual Property Strategy Headquarters 2019: 12)

The strategy emphasizes that in order for foreigners to 'discover the appeal' of Cool Japan contents, ranging from traditional culture to contemporary art and popular culture, it is important to 'connect contents from different fields and different eras to create a story/narrative'. At the same time, 'a story based on Japanese history, tradition, or culture' is effective in this regard (Intellectual Property Strategy Headquarters 2019: 12–13). This approach linking multiple different types of content through stories and narratives and packaging them for promotion is interesting because it is perfectly aligned with the above-mentioned Japan Heritage policy, a comprehensive conservation/utilization system for cultural heritage promoted by the Agency for Cultural Affairs.

In Japan, in the first 20 years of the twenty-first century the contents tourism policy and the cultural heritage conservation policy have realized a common goal of 'integration of resources/assets/properties' through 'stories/narratives based on history/tradition/culture' under the Cool Japan strategy. However, in the context of war-related contents tourism this has raised questions about how, when, and under what circumstances Japan's past wars can be considered effective in attracting tourists; and given how Japan's wars with neighbouring countries still sour diplomatic relations, whether popular culture representations of war, particularly Japan's twentieth-century wars, sit comfortably within the Cool Japan policy.

Conclusions

The evidence from the chapters that follow suggests that wars up to the Satsuma Rebellion (1877) in a domestic Japanese context and wars up to the Boshin War (1868–1869) in an international context can be relatively safely used within Japanese-produced popular culture entertainment and the Cool Japan policy. Furthermore, these works can and do trigger significant tourism phenomena. However, immediately after the Meiji Restoration, Japanese expansionism began. Remembrance of this period from 1869 triggers emotive responses, particularly in China and South Korea. This is why Chinese and Korean fans of Japanese pop culture can be fans of pre-1868 contents such as the online game *Tōken Ranbu* (Chapter 8) or anime connected to Shinsengumi (Chapter 10), and visit war-related sites as contents tourists in the spirit of Cool Japan. But as soon as such tourism becomes connected to modern imperialism, fans of Japanese pop culture become far more sensitive to national political issues stemming from Japanese imperialism (Chapter 15).

The sections that follow, therefore, fall into three main categories. Parts I and II (Chapters 2–10) cover the period to 1869. These case studies are largely uncontroversial in both domestic and international contexts. War can be depicted as entertaining and fans of any nationality can be contents tourists. Parts IV and V (Chapters 15–23) focus on the Asia-Pacific War onwards, a period when war- and military-related tourism remain highly politicized, but can assume entertainment aspects if distanced sufficiently from political controversy, or as a niche activity within a Japanese domestic context (such as kamikaze tourism – see Chapter 18; Seaton 2019b). Part III, meanwhile, is something of a transition period. Controversial issues exist, but they tend to be debated among limited numbers of people who are most affected, particularly those in the regions of Japan or abroad where there are tourist sites (such as those relating to the Russo-Japanese War, Chapter 12). However, regardless of the period there are always 'borders of memory' running through war-related sites and the potential for conflict between 'interpretative communities'. The implications of these conflicts and ways in which they may potentially be resolved are addressed in the concluding chapter of the book.

References

Agency for Cultural Affairs, n.d. *Japan heritage.* Agency for Cultural Affairs. https:// www.bunka.go.jp/seisaku/bunkazai/nihon_isan/pdf/nihon_isan_pamphlet _english.pdf.

Beeton, S., 2015. *Travel, tourism and the moving image*. Bristol: Channel View Publications.

Boyle, T., 2019. Borders of memory: affirmation and contestation over Japan's heritage. *Japan Forum*, 31 (3), 293–312.

Chronis, A., 2012. Between place and story: Gettysburg as tourism imaginary. *Annals of Tourism Research*, 39 (4), 1797–1816.

Figal, G., 2012. *Beachheads: war, peace, and tourism in postwar Okinawa*. Lanham: Rowman & Littlefield.

Fish, S., 2004. Interpretive communities. *In*: J. Rivkin and M. Ryan, eds. *Literary theory: an anthology*. 2nd ed. Maiden, MA: Blackwell Publishing, 217–221.

Gravari-Barbas, M. and Graburn, N., 2012. Tourist imaginaries. Via tourism review, 1. https://doi.org/10.4000/viatourism.1180.

Intellectual Property Strategy Headquarters, 2011. *Kūru Japan suishin ni kansuru akushon puran*. Prime Minister's Office of Japan. https://www.kantei.go.jp/jp/singi/titeki2/kettei/cjap.pdf.

Intellectual Property Strategy Headquarters, 2019. *Kūru Japan senryaku*. Cabinet Office. https://www.cao.go.jp/cool_japan/about/pdf/190903_cjstrategy.pdf.

Japan Tourism Agency, JNTO, Ministry of Economy, Trade and Industry, and JETRO, 2013. *Hōnichi gaikokujin zōka ni muketa kyōdō kōdō keikaku*. JETRO. https://www.jetro.go.jp/news/releases/20130620382-news/actionplan.pdf.

Kushner, B., 2006. *The thought war: Japanese imperial propaganda*. Honolulu: University of Hawai'i Press.

Lennon, J. and Foley, M., 2010. *Dark tourism: the attraction of death and disaster*. Andover: Cengage Learning.

Ministry of Land, Infrastructure & Transport; Ministry of Economy, Trade & Industry; and Agency for Cultural Affairs, 2005. *Eizō tō kontentsu no seisaku, katsuyō ni yoru chiiki shinkō no arikata ni kansuru chōsa hōkokusho*. MLIT. www.mlit.go.jp/kokudokeikaku/souhatu/h16seika/12eizou/12eizou.htm.

Reijnders, S., 2011. *Places of the imagination: media, tourism, culture*. Farnham, Surrey: Ashgate.

Rosenstone, R.A., 2000. Oliver Stone as historian. *In*: R.B. Toplin, ed. *Oliver Stone's USA: film, history, and controversy*. Lawrence: University Press of Kansas, 26–39.

Ruoff, K.J., 2014. Japanese tourism to Mukden, Nanjing, and Qufu, 1938–1943. *Japan Review*, 27, 171–200.

Seaton, P.A., 2007. *Japan's contested war memories: the 'memory rifts' in historical consciousness of World War II*. London: Routledge.

Seaton, P., 2019a. Islands of 'dark' and 'light/lite' tourism: war-related contents tourism around the Seto Inland Sea. *Japan Review*, 33, 299–327.

Seaton, P., 2019b. Kamikaze museums and contents tourism. *Journal of War & Culture Studies*, 12 (1), 67–84.

Seaton, P., Yamamura, T., Sugawa-Shimada, A. and Jang, K., 2017. *Contents tourism in Japan: pilgrimages to 'sacred sites' of popular culture*. New York: Cambria Press.

Thomson, A., 1994. *ANZAC memories: living with the legend*. Oxford: Oxford University Press.

Yamamura, T., 2020. Introduction: contents tourism beyond anime tourism. *In*: T. Yamamura and P. Seaton, eds. *Contents tourism and pop culture fandom*. Bristol: Channel View Publications, 1–16.

Yamamura, T. and Seaton, P., 2020. Tourism. *In*: H. Takeda and M. Williams, eds. *Routledge handbook of contemporary Japan*. London: Routledge, 401–412.

Zwigenberg, R., 2014. *Hiroshima: the origins of global memory culture*. Cambridge: Cambridge University Press.

Part I

From myths to the middle ages

2 The narrative worlds of ancient wars

Travelling heroes in *Kojiki*

Takayoshi Yamamura

The invention/adoption of writing in Japan was during the Nara era (710–794). This transition from pre-literate to literate society is regarded as the birth of written mythology and history in Japan (Sakamoto 2005: 2). It is also the dawn of the literary development of war-related contents. *Kojiki* (*Records of Ancient Matters*, AD 712) is a chronicle of myths and histories often regarded as 'the oldest book in Japan' (Kadokawa Shoten 2002: 3; Ō no Yasumaro, 2014). *Kojiki*'s purpose, as stated in its preface, was to 'explain the legitimacy of the emperor's rule' as ancient Japan became a nation (Sakamoto 2005: 7). *Kojiki*'s narrative world consists of epic stories that oscillate between myth and history. Consequently, *Kojiki* is often treated as a literary book rather than a history book, and many of the stories are familiar to people in modern Japan. Research on *Kojiki* began in earnest during the Edo period with the publication of Motoori Norinaga's *Kojiki-den* in 1798. Records of Motoori's March 1772 travel to Hatsuse (Hase), Yoshino and Yamato suggest that he went 'on a tour of the Imperial tombs for the purpose of writing *Kojiki-den*' (Hashimoto 2006: 13), meaning that contents tourism related to *Kojiki* probably transpired during the Edo period.

Kojiki contains numerous tales depicting battles fought by heroic deities and imperial families to slay monsters and to pacify the nation. Emperor Jimmu was Japan's first emperor and Yamato Takeru is the 'greatest hero of ancient history' (Sakamoto 2005: 42), who contributed to the pacification of the Japanese nation. Journeys in their footsteps are still practised in various ways today. For example, in September 2012, to commemorate the 1,300th anniversary of the compilation of *Kojiki*, the Miyazaki City Tourism Association held an event called 'Jimmu tennō go-tōsen kyanpēn' (Emperor Jimmu's conquest of the east campaign) inviting people to visit locations associated with Emperor Jimmu's eastward expedition. Participants departed from Miyazaki Jingu Shrine for a seven-day tour to Kashihara Jingu Shrine (Miyazaki nichinichi shinbun 2012). Kashihara Jingu was

DOI: 10.4324/9781003239970-3

built in 1890 at the eastern foot of Mt. Unebi in Nara prefecture, where it is said that the palace in which he unified the country and ascended the throne as Emperor Jimmu was located. Moreover, Wakayama Prefecture's official tourism website lists places associated with Emperor Jimmu and refers to 'Jimmu's far-reaching Eastern Expedition' (Wakayama Tourism Federation n.d.). Meanwhile, Kagoshima Prefecture's official tourism website introduces a 'power spot' at Kumaso no Ana (Cave of Kumaso), where chief Kawakamitakeru of the Kumaso (a people or region who are said to have resisted the Yamato kingship) lived before being conquered by Yamato Takeru (Kagoshima Prefectural Visitors Bureau n.d.).

However, in the section on Yamato Takeru in *Nihon minzoku daijiten* (the Japan Folk Encyclopaedia) it says,

> the hero Yamato Takeru did not actually exist in ancient times, but the history of armed struggle and confrontation that accompanied

Figure 2.1 The flag of Yata-garasu (mythical three-legged raven), Kumano Hongu Taisha Shrine. In *Kojiki*, there is a story that Yata-garasu guided Emperor Jimmu from Kumano in Wakayama to Kashihara in Yamato during Jimmu's eastern expedition. The shrine still cherishes this mythical story today. Author's photo.

the establishment of the ancient state (the Yamato Court) can be seen as somehow being projected in the conception of this heroic figure.
(Fukuta *et al.* 1999: 745).

Thus, the boundary between myths and historical facts is blurred, and archaeological and historical verification is often difficult. There are multiple interpretations of the narratives of *Kojiki* and whether the characters were real or not.

Ancient war narratives in the era of empire

In Japan today, this type of contents tourism centred on heroic battle stories in *Kojiki* is frequently positioned as a journey in search of the romance of ancient history, as seen in the expression 'Sites of ancient history evoking myth and romance' (*Shinwa to roman wo kakitateru kodaishi no butai*) on the cover of one guidebook introducing locations in *Kojiki* (Takarajimasha 2020). Mythological and spiritual images of the places are also promoted and consumed as 'power spots' rather than as war-related historical sites (e.g. Kagoshima Prefectural Visitors Bureau n.d.). However, these ancient war narratives became strongly linked to Japanese imperialism. Particularly from the Meiji period (1868–1912) onwards, the story of Emperor Jimmu, as the story of the first emperor, played a central role in the construction of the modern centralized state system. For example, 'the charismatic nationalist speaker Tanaka Chigaku' gave a lecture that was 'broadcast throughout the [Japanese] empire by radio in 1935' and 'drew comparison between the modern Imperial Army's heroic victory over its Russian foe at Port Arthur and Emperor Jimmu's earlier achievements' (Ruoff 2010: 133). Contents tourism following in his heroic footsteps became highly politicized. During the Second World War, the government announced 21 locations 'officially recognized as sacred sites relating to the first emperor', such as Kashihara Jingu Shrine, in order to boost national prestige (Ruoff 2010: 40–41). Stories surrounding these sacred sites were widely publicized and 'imperial heritage tourism' flourished (Ruoff 2010: 82–105). The culmination of this fervour and flow of people was a series of national events held on a nationwide scale in 1940 to commemorate the 2,600th anniversary of the enthronement of Emperor Jimmu.

Creating multi-voiced imaginaries

Another discourse, however, emphasizes the importance of reading *Kojiki* from the perspective of the conquered. *Kojiki* was compiled as a central history or a vision of the nation centred on the emperor, and it 'reflects political intentions as a national policy' (Shirakura 2004: 27). However, from the perspective of peripheral history, these heroic narratives in *Kojiki* are about the process by which 'indigenous peoples' were 'conquered' (Oguma 1995: 22). In recent years there have been academic attempts to present Yamato Takeru's eastern conquest of the Emishi (the ancient name for indigenous people inhabiting eastern and northern Japan) in *Kojiki* as a history of the centralization and control of indigenous peoples in the context of indigenous Ainu history (Hirotake 2012: 56–58), or as a move 'towards a multi-voiced history' (Katō 2012: 204). In this regard, although not inspired by *Kojiki*, contents tourism triggered by the manga/anime *Golden Kamuy* (Chapter 11), which presents both *Wajin* (ethnic Japanese) and Ainu perspectives, demonstrates the potential of developing contents tourism based on a multi-voiced imaginary with perspectives from both centre and periphery, conquerors and conquered.

There are several noteworthy postwar adaptations of the heroic tales of *Kojiki* with a multi-voiced perspective, although I have been unable to confirm whether these adaptations have triggered contents tourism. The manga by Tezuka Osamu, *Hi no Tori: Yamato-hen* (*Phoenix-Yamato*, 1968–1969, later developed into an anime and an opera), introduces a character based on Yamato Takeru and depicts in detail the king of Kumaso (indigenous people or region in ancient southern Kyushu) and his sister Kajika. Another film in the same vein, though not a direct adaptation of *Kojiki*, is Miyazaki Hayao's animated film *Princess Mononoke*. The 'historical setting' is 'a remote area of Japan in the Muromachi period' and 'the main character, a boy, is a descendant of the Emishi, who disappeared in ancient times after being overthrown by the Yamato regime' (Miyazaki 1996: 419–420).

Conclusion

The heroic tales in *Kojiki* blur the boundaries between historical facts and fiction, leaving them open to interpretation and stimulating the reader's imagination. In this context, *Kojiki* is akin to the ancient Greek epic poems *The Iliad* and *The Odyssey*, and the British *Arthurian romances*. The common denominator is that these contents in a heroic format have since been adapted in various ways and continue to generate contents tourism. Regarding ancient Japanese heroic tales, academic interest has often focused on the misuse of mythology and Shintoism by the military, especially before and during the Second World War (e.g. Ruoff

2010). However, multi-voiced contents including the viewpoints of the periphery and the conquered have also been produced in postwar Japan, despite the motifs of these heroic tales. Multi-voiced contents and tourism phenomena also exist in international and modern contexts, for example, *Daichi no Ko* (1995 – a Japan-China co-produced TV drama based on the novel by Yamasaki Toyoko depicting the life of a Japanese orphan who remained in China after Japan's defeat in 1945) and two films about the Battle of Iwo Jima directed by Clint Eastwood: *Flags of Our Fathers* (2006 – from the American perspective) and *Letters from Iwo Jima* (2006 – from the Japanese perspective). Despite their positioning as national myths, therefore, *Kojiki* and related contents tourism exemplify the temporal and historical consciousness (*rekishi ninshiki*) aspects of war-related contents tourism discussed in Chapter 1, namely the ways in which contents are continuously adapted and reworked over time within a national or cultural community; and in which national/cultural perspectives give rise to divergent interpretations of war-related contents.

References

Fukuta, A., Kanda, Y., Shintani, T., Nakagomi, M., Yukawa, Y. and Watanabe, Y., eds, 1999. *Nihon minzoku daijiten (jō)*. Tokyo: Yoshikawa Kōbunkan.

Hashimoto, M., 2006. Motoori Norinaga no Yamato: 'Sugagasa-nikki' to 'Kojiki-den' (pure Man'yō no tabi toshite). *Annual Report of Man'yo Historical Research*, 4, 10–19.

Hirotake, R., 2012. Kodai 'Emishi' wo meguru seido to jittai. *In*: H. Katō and K. Suzuki, eds. *Atarashī Ainu-shi no kōchiku: senshi-hen kodai-hen chūsei-hen*. Sapporo: Center for Ainu and Indigenous Studies, Hokkaido University, 52–61.

Kadokawa Shoten, ed., 2002. *Beginner's classics Kojiki*. Tokyo: Kadokawa Bunko.

Kagoshima Prefectural Visitors Bureau, n.d. *Kumaso no ana*. Kagoshima Prefectural Visitors Bureau. https://www.kagoshima-kankou.com/s/spot/10134/.

Katō, H., 2012. Matome. *In*: H. Katō and K. Suzuki, eds. *Atarashī Ainu-shi no kōchiku: senshi-hen kodai-hen chūsei-hen*. Sapporo: Center for Ainu and Indigenous Studies, Hokkaido University, 203–213.

Miyazaki, H., 1996. *Shuppatsu-ten 1979–1996*. Tokyo: Tokuma Shoten.

Miyazaki nichinichi shinbun, 2012. Kojiki hensan 1300 nen Miyazaki: [dai 5-bu] Jinmu-sama tōsei dōkō-kikō. *Miyazaki nichinichi shinbun*, 11 September. https://www.the-miyanichi.co.jp/tokushu/category_129/.

Ō no Yasumaro (trans. Gustav Heldt), 2014. *Kojiki: an account of ancient matters*. New York: Columbia University Press.

Oguma, E., 1995. *Tan'itsu minzoku shinwa no kigen: 'Nihon-jin' no jigazō no kēfu*. Tokyo: Shinyosha.

Ruoff, K.J., 2010. *Imperial Japan at its zenith: the wartime celebration of the empire's 2,600th anniversary*. Ithaca: Cornell University Press.

Sakamoto, M., 2005. *Zusetsu chizu to arasuji de yomu Kojiki to Nihonshoki*. Tokyo: Seishun Publishing.

Shirakura, S., 2004. *Hīrō to seigi*. Tokyo: Kodomo no miraisha.

Takarajimasha, ed., 2020. *Kojiki/Nihonshoki shinwa wo tabi suru*. Tokyo: Takarajimasha.

Wakayama Tourism Federation, n.d. *Wakayama Ki-ki no tabi: Jinmu-tōsei Harukanaru Tenka-taihei no Michi*. Wakayama Prefecture Official Tourism. https://www.wakayama-kanko.or.jp/features/journey-of-ancient-chronicles/story03/.

3 The Mongol invasions of Japan and Tsushima tourism

Kyungjae Jang

Tsushima Island lies in the straits between South Korea and Japan, approximately halfway between Busan and Fukuoka. This strategically important island has been a staging post for Korean–Japanese exchange and trade for centuries but also a site of various wars: the Battle of Tsushima Straits during the Russo-Japanese War, the 1592 and 1597 Japanese invasions of Korea (when the island was a forward staging post), a Korean invasion in 1419 to curb the activities of *wakō* pirates, and the Mongol invasions of 1274 and 1281, known as *Genkō* in Japanese. Kublai Khan (1215–1294), the first emperor of the Yuan Dynasty, attempted to invade Japan twice, along with the already colonised Goryeo Dynasty on the Korean Peninsula (Turnbull 2010: 6). This was the first large-scale attack by outside forces on the Japanese archipelago. Japanese warriors struggled in the face of the Mongols' gunpowder weapons. Even so, strong Japanese resistance led to protracted war. Both invasions were ended abruptly by typhoons (the *kamikaze*, divine winds) and have assumed an important position in early Japanese history and national mythology.

On 8 November 2020, the Genkō Summit was held in Matsuura city on mainland Kyushu. It was attended by the mayors of Tsushima and Iki (another island halfway between Tsushima and Matsuura), which were the two main sites of fighting during the Mongol invasions. The three municipalities produced a joint declaration to utilize their shared history of the invasions for the purpose of tourism promotion. Previously, the Mongol invasions had barely been used as a tourism resource and with only minimal success. There has been a small Mongol Invasions Museum (Genkō shiryōkan) in Fukuoka since 1904, and a Mongol Village in Matsuura opened in 1993, but then closed in 2016 (the grounds are now a free-to-enter park). The reason for the new joint declaration was the release of two works of popular culture that have raised considerably expectations for Mongol-invasion-related tourism: the manga/anime

DOI: 10.4324/9781003239970-4

Angorumoa: Genkō kassen-ki (*Angolmois: record of Mongol invasion*, 2013–)
and the PlayStation game *Ghost of Tsushima* (2020).

Entertainmentization of the Mongol invasions

The Mongol invasions have long been depicted in popular culture, such
as movies and dramas. Many representations draw on *Mōko shūrai ekotoba*
(*Illustrated Account of the Mongol Invasion*, Figure 3.1), a set of two illustrated handscrolls from the late Kamakura period (1185–1333). They
are said to have been painted in the 1290s by order of the *gokenin* (vassal
of the shogunate) Takezaki Suenaga, who fought during the invasions.
As illustrations commissioned by a warlord who participated directly in
the war, *Mōko shūrai ekotoba* is typically reproduced in most elementary,
junior high, and high school history textbooks and was designated as a
national treasure in 2021.

Manga artist Takagi Nanahiko is the author of *Angolmois*. His ten-vol-
ume manga (2013–2018) was set in Tsushima in 1274 and was adapted
into a TV anime with 12 episodes in 2018. From 2019 onwards, season
two of the manga began about the Hakata invasion, an entirely fictional
storyline in which the hero Kuchi sneaks aboard a Goryeo dynasty ship
and fights in Hakata, Fukuoka. Takagi acknowledges the role of *Mōko
shūrai ekotoba* in his creative process:

> The text was difficult and I could not understand it at all, but just
> following the pictures was interesting. There were many kinds of
> battles on land, at sea, using gunpowder weapons … Hearing about
> the Mongol invasions in class [at school] did not make much of an
> impact, but thanks to the handscrolls I had fascinating material to
> work with.
>
> (Aou 2015)

Figure 3.1 A section from the *Illustrated Account of the Mongol Invasion*. Source: Kyushu
University Library (n.d.)

He created a prototype of the manga based on the handscrolls prior to *Angolmois*. However, publishers rejected it for lack of 'entertainment' value. Learning from that failure, he made *Angolmois* more entertaining by using many fictional characters (Aou 2015). This relates to issues discussed in Chapter 1 about how war memories transform into entertainment. *Mōko shūrai ekotoba* is a realistic record of war experiences, and contents based faithfully on such historic texts are inevitably inferior as entertainment. The entertainmentization of war memories requires that they are 'edited, interpreted, and rewritten with reference to the contemporary cultural milieu' (Chapter 1). Consequently, the *Angolmois* plot includes loyalty and betrayal, and characters have secret or special abilities that do not appear in actual history but have entertainment value. Some characters are purely fictional, for example, the heroine is a princess of Tsushima who did not exist in actual history. She commands the exiled samurai who live in Tsushima to fight for the island.

Meanwhile, *Ghost of Tsushima* is set during the same 1274 Mongol invasion of Tsushima. Released in July 2020, it is an open world action-adventure game in which the protagonist is a samurai who resists the invasion. The game attracted attention for its detailed artwork in a production announcement video shown at Paris Games Week in 2017. The game sold 2.4 million copies worldwide in three days after release and had sold 6.5 million copies by March 2021, when a film adaptation was announced (Fox 2021). *Ghost of Tsushima*, like *Angolmois*, is based on historical events but is completely fictional. The game is in the Chanbara (sword fighting) genre and all the characters are fictional, too, which distances the game from history. The main character, Sakai Jin, is the only surviving samurai after all other samurais on Tsushima Island are wiped out on Komoda Beach by the invading Mongols. In actual history, this battle (in 1274) also ended in a one-sided victory for the Mongols, but in the game Sakai fights on.

The game takes place in an open world with Tsushima Island as the background. There is a high degree of freedom of movement. The main character can visit most of the island, and players fight while visiting natural locations, villages, castles, and shrines as if they were actually travelling on Tsushima. Furthermore, the user interface was excluded from the screen as much as possible so that players could be immersed in the locations. This creates an atmosphere that can lead people to the real space, Tsushima.

Contents tourism in Tsushima

While Takagi's manga raised domestic interest in the Mongol invasions, *Ghost of Tsushima* raised expectations of new forms of international tourism in the post-COVID-19 era. Tsushima is where the Mongols invaded first and is on the periphery of Japan. In fact, it is closer to Korea than the main islands of Japan, so the proportion of Korean tourists is high. In 2018, before the COVID-19 pandemic, nearly 300,000 of the island's 418,000 overnight guests were Koreans, accounting for 75 percent of total guests and 99 percent of foreign guests (Nagasaki Prefecture Tourism Promotion Division n.d.). However, this dependence on Koreans for Tsushima tourism poses risks. There was a boycott of tourism in Japan by Koreans in 2019 due to a worsening diplomatic row over contemporary historical issues (a tit-for-tat trade row flared followed by a ruling by a Korean court to seize Japanese corporate assets to compensate colonial-era forced labourers). In addition, the travel patterns of Korean tourists, usually short visits and minimal consumption, were also problems in Tsushima tourism.

In this context, the municipality is trying to revitalize tourism through collaboration with the content producers. In 2018, when the *Angolmois* anime was produced, in cooperation with the production company a pre-broadcast screening of one episode was held at the Tsushima City Exchange Center to inform residents of the existence of the anime. Since 2019, Tsushima has been selected every year as one of 88 Japanese anime spots designated by the Anime Tourism Association. However, the distance of Tsushima from mainland Japan and the time required to get there can put off many travellers.

For *Ghost of Tsushima*, in collaboration with Tsushima City, a special webpage was created to provide foreign tourists with information on related places appearing in the game, albeit without discussing tourism directly. However, the year of the game's release was also when the COVID-19 'invasion' occurred. The game's effects on tourism post-COVID-19 must be a subject for future research. Nevertheless, the potential is reflected in the Mayor's decision to name game director Nate Fox and creative director Jason Connell as permanent tourism ambassadors in March 2021 (Nichols 2021).

Conclusions

These two recent works about the Mongol invasions constitute interesting examples of turning war memories into entertainment and tourism resources. The entertainmentization of the invasions is made possible by the free interpretation and use of history. While the invasions happened in East Asia, a place that is politically and diplomatically divided over more recent issues of invasion and war, more than 700 years have passed since the Mongol invasions. Direct stakeholders no longer exist. Furthermore, the Yuan and Goryeo dynasties, and the shogunate, have little bearing on current national politics. The fact that the contents depict a war with an indecisive conclusion due to the intervention of nature also plays a part in reducing political sensitivity.

Even so, the entertainmentization of war history and subsequent increase in the attractiveness of the region for travellers are characteristics of war-related contents tourism. *Mōko shūrai ekotoba* inspired the creation of manga and anime, and a game based on the period gave the region more international appeal. In other circumstances, this chapter could have been about tourism revitalization induced by popular culture in Tsushima in 2020. Due to the pandemic, however, the story of contents tourism on Tsushima is, for now, encapsulated in another question one often hears asked regarding history and wars in an entertainment context: What if …?

References

Aou, K., 2015. *Interview with Nanahiko Takagi, 'Angorumoa genkō kassen-ki'*. Natasha, Inc. https://natalie.mu/comic/pp/angolmois_comic.

Fox, N., 2021. *Sucker Punch Productions provides first details on the Sony Pictures film, being directed by Chad Stahelski*. Europe, Sony Interactive Entertainment. https://blog.playstation.com/2021/03/25/a-ghost-of-tsushima-movie-is-in-the-works/.

Kyushu University Library, n.d. *Kichō shiryō (Kyūdai korekushon): Mōko shūrai ekotoba*. Kyushu University Library. https://guides.lib.kyushu-u.ac.jp/c.php?g=774839&p=5560026.

Nagasaki Prefecture Tourism Promotion Division, n.d. *Tourism statistics of Nagasaki Prefecture 2018*. Nagasaki City, Nagasaki Prefectural. https://www.pref.nagasaki.jp/bunrui/kanko-kyoiku-bunka/kanko-bussan/statistics/kankoutoukei/296549.html.

Nichols, D., 2021. *Ghost of Tsushima directors become permanent tourism ambassadors for Tsushima island*. Gamerant. https://gamerant.com/ghost-tsushima-directors-become-permanent-tourism-ambassadors-tsushima-island/.

Turnbull, S., 2010. *The Mongol invasions of Japan 1274 and 1281*. Oxford: Osprey Publishing.

4 *Sekiro: Shadows Die Twice* and contents tourism in Aizu-Wakamatsu

Aleksandra Jaworowicz-Zimny

Sekiro: Shadows Die Twice is an action-adventure video game developed by FromSoftware. It was one of the most popular games of 2019, selling over 2 million copies in ten days after its release (Baird 2019). Set in a fantasy version of Warring States (Sengoku, 1467–1590) period Japan, players fight as one-armed *shinobi* Sekiro against the Ashina clan. The player must protect Kuro, a boy of an ancient bloodline with magical powers, who has been targeted by the clan. The plot features magical rituals and mythical creatures, and the map of *Sekiro*'s world does not faithfully represent Japan's geography. Fantasy realms, however, do not stop fans from identifying real-life inspirations for the game.

Japanese gaming forums and blogs contain discussions about the game's historical inspirations and real-life locations. Players usually first link the game to Fukushima prefecture, not only because of the snowy mountain landscape but also because of the name 'Ashina'. In the game, Ashina Isshin is the founder of the clan and leader of a small, sovereign state. Ashina's land is being invaded by a military power called the Interior Ministry (*Daifu*). Fan theories are almost unanimous in identifying the Aizu branch of the historical Ashina clan, who were rulers of the Aizu region during the Muromachi period (approx. 1336–1573), as the real-life model for the in-game Ashina. Many fans go one step further and identify Ashina Isshin as loosely based on Ashina Moriuji (1521–1580) (Luggage_Z 2019), who managed to unify most of the Aizu area under his rule (Aizu-Wakamatsu Kankō Byūrō n.d.). Ashina was never a particularly influential clan, so the amount of information that can be exchanged by fans is limited. Twitter user Kagura, who is a Sengoku period enthusiast and *Sekiro* fan, admits that despite her interest in history she did not know much about the Ashina clan – just enough to connect the name to Aizu-Wakamatsu. The game motivated her to research more about local history and the inspiration behind the characters. She discovered events seemingly reflected in the game: conflicts

DOI: 10.4324/9781003239970-5

between the Ashina and Tamura clans, and Date Masamune's invasion of the Fukushima region (Kagura 2021). Fans name the 1589 Battle of Suriagehara as connected somehow to the game since it was the biggest conflict in the area during that period. Some even interpret the plot as 'alternate history', showing what could have been if the Ashina clan won the battle (Diggu 2020). Such online debates suggest that some fans enjoy the hunt for even vague historical references. Nevertheless, accounts of those who visited places related to the historical Ashina suggest that their primary aim was to discover the world of *Sekiro* more fully, and learning actual Sengoku history remains only in the background.

The centre of the Ashina's military power was Kurokawa Castle, today known as Aizu-Wakamatsu or Tsuruga Castle. Originally built by Ashina Naomori in 1384, the castle remained in the hands of the Ashina until 1589. Numerous players express interest in potential links between the in-game Ashina Castle and the historical Ashina clan's residence. However, despite the game being set in the Sengoku period, the huge in-game castle complex reflects the design of an Early Modern period castle. Such images of Japanese castles are widespread in popular culture, but given the game's timeline, this representation is an anachronism (see Chapter 9). The in-game castle is not modelled on any specific real-life building but is a fantasy location firmly rooted in the image of an Edo period castle.

Aizu-Wakamatsu Castle was reconstructed in 1965 in its form from 1639 when it served as a residence of the Katō clan. Since Aizu-Wakamatsu Castle today has Edo period architecture, it shares with in-game Ashina Castle various characteristics, like the keep and stone walls. It does not need to look exactly like the fortress in the game, but as the castle is linked to the real-life Ashina clan, it becomes the real-world counterpart of Ashina Castle for many fans. One fan who visited Aizu-Wakamatsu in March 2020 refers to it as *seichi (mōsō) junrei*, '(fantasy) sacred site pilgrimage', at a place that is not specifically portrayed in the work, but physically represents the core of the narrative (Mizunomi Byakushō 2020).

The lack of real-life game locations does not prevent *Sekiro* fans from looking at the castle complex through the lens of the game. Mizunomi Byakushō regularly mentions game elements during his walk around Tsuruga Castle. For example, the remains of the entrance gate call to mind the terrifying demon guard, and the fosse looks like a place where the Headless (*Kubinashi*) monster hides. Similarly, Kagura, who went to Tsuruga Castle, declared the castle a 'sacred site' (Loc_cos 2019). Even though she had been to Tsuruga Castle before, the post-*Sekiro* visit allowed her to notice new elements. For example, in the game *tsukimi yagura*, the 'moon viewing tower', plays an important role in the opening sequences. During her '*Sekiro* pilgrimage' Kagura noticed for the first time that Tsuruga Castle used to have a *tsukimi yagura* in the past – the tower's location is now marked with a commemorative stone (Kagura 2021). Hence, Tsuruga Castle can be rediscovered through the comparison with its counterpart in *Sekiro*, even if the connection is mainly through the name of Ashina.

It is not possible for *Sekiro* fans in Aizu-Wakamatsu to take pictures of exact spots from the game, like pilgrims visiting sacred sites of other franchises often do. Nevertheless, Twitter users have posted '*Sekiro* impression' photographs recreating the general style and atmosphere of *Sekiro* visuals. Kagura, for example, shot close-ups of the white castle tower and posted a picture of herself kneeling in a *shinobi*-inspired pose on the wall (Figure 4.1).

During their pilgrimages, fans can also spot references to the game outside the castle. Many result from likenesses in names or the usage of kanji characters. Local *azuki* bean sweets are called 'Tomoe monaka', and Tomoe is one of the characters in *Sekiro*. Kagura recommended the sweets and tweeted, '[If you're a fan], you'll buy it just for its name' (Loc_cos 2019). In another example, locally made Tatsuizumi liquor, written

Figure 4.1 A fan creates a '*Sekiro* illusion' by making a *shinobi*-pose against the backdrop of Aizu-Wakamatsu Castle. Photo courtesy of Kagura, @ Loc_cos.

with a kanji meaning 'dragon', resembles the in-game Dragonspring *sake* (rice wine, written with a different kanji of the same meaning); and a restaurant called Jūmonji-ya shares its name with one of Ashina Isshin's sword techniques, *jūmonji-giri*, 'cross attack' (Mizunomi Byakushō 2020).

The similarity in settings can also trigger visitors' imaginations. Aizu Ashinomaki *onsen* (hot spring) is located deep in the mountains by a river. This place brings to fans' minds the magical Rejuvenating Waters, especially since the place is marked with a big sign informing visitors of the *onsen*'s link to the Ashina clan (Kagura 2021). The Aizu-Wakamatsu area did not need to directly inspire the game's art to be perceived by fans as a physical representation of *Sekiro*'s world. Such 'fantasy pilgrimage', however, seems to be less prevalent than a pilgrimage to places accurately portrayed in works of popular culture. Tsuruga Castle management did not notice a major increase in visitor numbers after the game's premiere. They were not aware of *Sekiro* and its links to Aizu-Wakamatsu until asked directly by the author. This suggests the game's limited impact on tourism in the area (albeit under the severe restrictions on movement caused by the COVID-19 pandemic) in comparison to, for example, Shinsengumi-themed works. Since the castle was the site of a Boshin War battle in 1868, fans of franchises centred on Shinsengumi, like *Rurouni Kenshin* or *Hakuoki* (Chapters 10 and 14) are frequent castle visitors according to the castle's management (personal correspondence, 2 April 2021).

The game's producer, FromSoftware, has never confirmed any links between the game and the region. Furthermore, unlike *Ghost of Tsushima* (Chapter 3), there are no municipal initiatives or cooperation with game producers to promote the Aizu region. Still, some of the distributor's decisions may be seen as an acknowledgement of Aizu-Wakamatsu's importance. *Sekiro* pre-release try-outs were organized at various stores across the country. As Twitter user Tamori noticed, in the case of Fukushima prefecture the bigger cities like Fukushima or Koriyama would seem more obvious choices, but the try-out took place at the GEO store in Aizu-Wakamatsu. Tamori explains this decision via the Ashina clan's link to the location (tamori_DX 2019).

Sekiro generates not only 'fantasy pilgrimage'. Some game locations are inspired by real-life places across Japan. Tōfuku-ji Temple in Kyoto and Itsukushima Shrine in Hiroshima prefecture are considered 'sacred spots' by game fans since they seemingly inspired the in-game Sempō Temple bridge and Fountainhead Palace, respectively (ot_Kapoor 2019; suna_game 2019). According to YouTube user Love Thieves, over 30 real-life places that inspired game locations can be named (Love Thieves 2019). Twitter debates suggest that some *Sekiro* fans either visited or are planning to visit places visually represented in the game. But Ashina Castle remains central to fans' imaginations and is the predominant theme in online discussions concerning 'sacred sites'.

In summary, *Sekiro* is a fictional narrative set in a fantasy world, and this narrative is what primarily captures fans' attention. Even if the fantasy world is not strictly modelled on Japanese landscapes, it still has the potential to generate real-life tourism. 'Fantasy pilgrimage' to Aizu-Wakamatsu cannot provide fans with physical representations of the game's visuals, but it allows them to interact with the symbol of *Sekiro*'s core narrative – the rise and fall of the Ashina clan. Trips by fans and research related to the game become opportunities to learn more about Sengoku period events in the Aizu region. However, the focus of fans' online debates and comments suggests that knowledge about Ashina leaders or the Battle of Suriagehara is primarily a collection of curiosities enriching the game's lore in the eyes of dedicated fans.

References

Aizu-Wakamatsu Kankō Byūrō, n.d. *Sawara/Ashina-shi jidai (Kamakura jidai – muromachi jidai) gaiyō*. Aizu-Wakamatsu. https://www.tsurugajo.com/history/asina.html.

Baird, S., 2019. Sekiro: shadows die twice has already sold more than 2 million copies in under 10 days. *The Gamer*, 12 April. https://www.thegamer.com/sekiro-shadows-die-twice-sold-more-2-million-copies-10-days/.

Diggu, A., 2020. *Rekishi IF mono toshite no Sekiro – Ashina-shi to Ashina-shi*. Note, 2 April. https://note.com/digarmor/n/n6ee4bf07660a.

Kagura (@Loc_cos), 5 June 2021. Twitter message to Aleksandra Jaworowicz-Zimny (@AleksandraZimny).

Loc_cos, 2019. Tweet, 25 October. https://twitter.com/loc_cos/status/1187643935566381058.

Love Thieves, 2019. *Sekiro real life locations*. YouTube. https://www.youtube.com/watch?v=YmNloDNKN-I.

Luggage_Z, 2019. Tweet, 18 April. https://twitter.com/luggage_z/status/1118716997720633344.

Mizunomi Byakushō, 2020. *Sekiro seichi (mōsō) junrei tsūringu 2020 3-gatsu*. Note, 25 March. https://note.com/mizunomihyakusyo/n/nce20b10c3a99.

ot_Kapoor, 2019. Tweet, 19 July. https://twitter.com/ot_kapoor/status/1152026274958675968.

suna_game, 2019. Tweet, 28 October. https://twitter.com/suna__game/status/1188798983889489922.

tamori_DX, 2019. Tweet, 25 March. https://twitter.com/tamori_DX/status/1110114385840607232.

5   History girls and women's war-related contents tourism

Akiko Sugawa-Shimada

Rekijo ('history girls') refers to young female (*joshi*) fans of history (*reki-shi*). Since the early 2000s, several anime, manga, and videogames have featured handsome young male characters modelled on actual historical figures/events. Consuming this history for women has become equivalent to consuming history-based popular culture. The Japanese media described such women's perceived 'gender crossover' into a formerly 'male' interest using the catchy term *rekijo*. Pop culture works have prompted young female fans to visit related sites such as birthplaces and graves of actual historical figures, battlefields, festivals, and museums in a phenomenon that clearly meets the criteria of contents tourism (Sugawa-Shimada 2015: 39). This chapter discusses history-based popular culture, especially about the Warring States (Sengoku) period, 1467–1590, and contents tourism by *rekijo* by examining Kuwabara Mizuna's light novel *Mirage of Blaze* series (1990–2004; spin-off works 2007–2017) and Capcom's video game *Sengoku BASARA* series (2005–present).

The *rekijo* phenomenon became relatively visible in the 2000s because Internet blogs and social media platforms (including Facebook, Twitter, Instagram, and Japanese social media platform mixi) enabled online interaction among anonymous users. However, female history fans existed before the term *rekijo* was coined. One representative example is fans of the *Mirage of Blaze* series, a psychic action fantasy novel for young readers featuring handsome young male characters based on samurai feudal lords (*daimyō*) of the Warring States period. The series was adapted into multiple formats: CD dramas (1992–1997), TV anime (2002), original animation video (2004), manga comics (2001; remake 2021), and theatre performances (2014–2018). Fans have travelled sites related to the stories since the 1990s. They were dubbed '*mirajennu*'[1] and their tourism was called the 'mirage tour' (Hashimoto 2006).

The story is set in 1990s Japan. The protagonist, Ōgi Takaya, is an ordinary but disobedient high school boy in Matsumoto city, Nagano.

DOI: 10.4324/9781003239970-6

One day a man in black, Naoe Nobutsuna, appears before Takaya and tells him that his true identity is Uesugi Kagetora, the first adopted son of Uesugi Kenshin.[2] In actual history, Kagetora was driven to kill himself by *seppuku* at the Battle of Otate (1578) for fighting against Uesugi Kagekatsu, his stepbrother, over their inheritance after their father's death. Based on these historical events and the ancient Japanese belief in vengeful spirits (*onryō*), in *Mirage of Blaze* Kagetora turns into a furious vengeful spirit after his death. However, Kenshin designates Kagetora as the leader of all exorcists to subdue other vengeful spirits with esoteric Buddhist power. The spirits of Kagetora and his four followers, nicknamed *yasha-shū* (demons), have survived by possessing human bodies for over 400 years. But Kagetora lost his memory after a battle against Oda Nobunaga in the 1950s. However, in 1990 numerous vengeful spirits of 'losers' in the Warring States period, including the surviving Oda Nobunaga, resume taking vengeance called 'Dark Sengoku'. Takaya/Kagetora is caught up in it with the *yasha-shū*. Meanwhile, Takaya/Kagetora recovers his memories and discovers that in his previous battle against Nobunaga, Naoe snatched the soul of Kagetora's girlfriend in order to transfer Kagetora's soul from his dying human body to her body. Naoe did it because 'he deeply loves Kagetora'. In addition to the thrilling storyline based on historical facts and its many action scenes, therefore, large numbers of *mirajenne* were absorbed in Naoe and Kagetora's love–hate relationship with its Boys' Love connotations.[3]

Wars and battles in the *Mirage of Blaze* series are fantasized to provide a site where Takaya/Kagetora recovers from his identity crisis and deep distrust of human beings. They are also used as backdrops to the story about love and hatred between Takaya/Kagetora and Naoe. Moved by the story, *mirajenne* went on 'mirage tours' to 'sacred sites' of the series in Nagano, Miyagi, Tokushima, Yamaguchi, and Kumamoto, and also sites and events related to historical figures on whom the protagonists were modelled, such as the ruins of Samegao Castle in Niigata (where Uesugi Kagetora killed himself) and Yonezawa Uesugi Festival in Yonezawa city, Yamagata prefecture.

Yonezawa Uesugi Festival started as a Shinto spring celebration when Uesugi Kagekatsu started ruling Dewa province after the Battle of Sekigahara in 1600. The 'mock battle' performance of the (Fourth) Battle of Kawanakajima (1561) between Kenshin and Takeda Shingen (feudal lord of Kai province, today Yamanashi prefecture) has been held since 1905. Yonezawa is not the actual battlefield, but Yonezawa Shrine, which enshrines Kenshin, allowed it to take place there. During the Asia-Pacific War (1937–1945), the mock battle performance was used as propaganda (Yonezawa Uesugi Festival Committee 2008). After 1945 the mock battles were cancelled, but following the hit NHK Taiga drama *Ten to chi to* (1969), the mock battle was restarted in 1973. In the 1990s, *mirajenne* besieged this performance and photographed the performers who played characters appearing in *Mirage of Blaze* (Figure 5.1).

Local residents performed the main roles in the Battle of Kawanakajima during the initial stages of the mirage tour phenomenon, so *mirajennes'* enthusiasm boosted local pride and identity. A local brewer collaborated with a local college to produce a wine as a souvenir for *mirajenne* called *chigiri* (noose), which was a reference to Naoe (Hashimoto 2006: 179). Visitation to the festival also enabled *mirajennes* to have off-line meetings with other *mirajennes* (Drian no sasayaki 2007). Thus, contents tourism related to *Mirage of Blaze* generated sociocultural impacts on the Yonezawa Uesugi Festival and helped revitalize the local economy.

Similar phenomena can be observed in contents tourism related to Ishida Mitsunari. Mitsunari was the closest subordinate of Toyotomi

Figure 5.1 Two *mirajennes* with a performer who played Irobe Katsunaga. He was Kenshin's military commissioner in actual history and a Kagetora follower in the novel. Author's photo.

Hideyoshi and was executed because he lost the Battle of Sekigahara against Tokugawa Ieyasu in 1600. The Tokugawa shogunate treated him as the rebel leader and destroyed Mitsunari's hometown Ishida village (today Ishida town, Shiga prefecture). Thereafter, villagers concealed their identities and hid the Ishida family graves from the Tokugawa authorities. However, in 1941 the tombstones of the Ishida clan were discovered underground at Hachiman Shrine (now Ishida Shrine). The Association in Honor of Ishida Mitsunari was created, which built a memorial building, Ishida Hall, at his birthplace and erected a statue near the Hall.

Initially, there were only two or three tourists a month (Asahi Shinbun 2009). Tourist flows changed drastically around 2010 after the first anime adaptation of the video game *Sengoku BASARA* was broadcast. Mitsunari is characterized as a young, crazy *ikemen* (hunk) who fanatically admires Hideyoshi. Negative images of Mitsunari as a conspirator and loser were swept away by this anime and two NHK Taiga dramas, *Tenchijin* (2009) and *Go* (2011), which depicted Mitsunari as a loyal samurai and casted popular young actors to play the role of Mitsunari. Visitor numbers per year to Ishida town in search of Mitsunari sites increased to over 1,000 around 2009, and approximately 90 percent of them were women (Asahi Shinbun 2009). Visitation by *rekijo* to Ishida town motivated young residents to revalue Mitsunari as a local brand. When I visited Ishida Hall in 2012, the chairman of the Association in Honor of Ishida Mitsunari, Kinoshita Shigeaki, told me that young residents of Ishida town were unwilling to support the Ishida Festival (held each November for Mitsunari's death day), but the number of young women visiting Ishida was motivating them to host tourists. The festival committee also relies on the participation of *rekijo* and they recruit 20 female volunteers from the Ishida Mitsunari Supporters' Club (Ishida Festival Committee 2016). The contents tourism of *rekijo* facilitates the generation of townspeople's local identity and enhances local pride.

Ishida Mitsunari is also used as a 'character' to promote Shiga prefecture. Shiga Prefecture set up the 'Ishida Mitsunari x Shiga portal site' (http://mitsunari.biwako-visitors.jp) in which Mitsunari appears as an anime-like character. It runs parodic videos on YouTube suggesting how Mitsunari was a loyal and talented governor, and how the image of Mitsunari was distorted by the victors of the Battle of Sekigahara. Meanwhile, Gifu prefecture, where Sekigahara is located, opened the Sekigahara Memorial (a large interactive facility with a museum) on 21 October 2020, the 420th anniversary of the Battle of Sekigahara. The banner above the entrance has the crests of Ishida Mitsunari and Tokugawa Ieyasu side by side.

Although it is named the Sekigahara Memorial, the museum's special exhibitions cover a variety of themes. In 2020, when the NHK Taiga drama featured Akechi Mitsuhide (who killed Oda Nobunaga at Honnō-ji Temple in 1582), a special exhibition about him was held, even though he also died in 1582, well before the Battle of Sekigahara. A special exhibition of Japanese swords was also held in 2020, probably because of the 'swords boom' among *rekijo* induced by the video-game/anime/play *Tōken Ranbu* (Chapter 8). In the summer of 2021, a Mitsunari special exhibition was held.

In summary, the Battle of Kawanakajima, Battle of Sekigahara and historical figures in the Warring States period have been popularized via history-based popular culture. They have attracted many young women, called *rekijo*, whose enthusiasm and contents tourism have contributed to the revitalization of Yonezawa and Ishida towns, both economically and socioculturally. The phenomenon also provides a different way of viewing history, that is, history as seen from the perspectives of 'losers'.

Notes

1 *Mirajennu* combines 'mirage' with the French suffix -enne, as in Parisienne. Members of the all-female Takarazuka Revue theatre troupe are called *takarajennu* and this inspired the term *mirajennu*.
2 Uesugi Kenshin was a strong feudal lord who ruled Echigo province (today's Niigata prefecture) in the late sixteenth century.
3 Boys' Love is a manga/anime genre targeting women which deals with male homosexual relationships.

References

Asahi shinbun, 2009. Oshiyoseru rekijo: gēmu de jinbutsuzō ni kyōkan. *Asahi shinbun*, 20 May, p. 25.
Drian no sasayaki, 2007. *Honō no mirage kikō 2007 Uesugi matsuri repōto mikkame!* http://make-only-one.seesaa.net/article/370069590.html.
Hashimoto, H., 2006. Matsuri: tsukurareru tabi. *In*: T. Oguchi, ed. *Kankō no shakai shinrigaku*. Kyoto: Kitaojishobo, 167–183.
Ishida Festival Committee, 2016. *Ishihaku no oshirase*. Ishida Mitsunari Festival. https://ameblo.jp/mitsunarisaijikko/entry-12481271518.html.
Sugawa-Shimada, A., 2015. *Rekijo*, pilgrimage and 'pop-spiritualism': pop-culture-induced heritage tourism of/for women. *Japan Forum*, 27 (1), 37–58.
Yonezawa Uesugi Festival Committee, 2008. *Kawanakajima kassen no rekishi*. Yonezawa Uesugi Matsuri homepage. http://uesugi.yonezawa-matsuri.jp/log/?l =350454.

Part II
The rise and fall of the Tokugawas

6 Satsuma's invasion of the Ryukyu Kingdom in 1609 and Okinawa tourism

Kyungjae Jang

Cultural anthropologist Sasaki Toshikazu speaks of the Japanese archipelago (Nihon rettō) as 'one archipelago, two countries, and three cultures' (Sasaki 2011: 70), namely one geographical collection of islands, a country with an emperor (Japan) and a country with a king (the Ryukyu Kingdom, until 1879), and the three cultures of Ainu, ethnic Japanese, and Ryukyuan. Through this expression, Sasaki argues for the need to recognize the coexistence of multiple cultures within the contemporary Japanese state and criticises the prevalent discourse of Japan as a mono-ethnic nation-state.

As Sasaki argues, the Ryukyu Kingdom – currently Okinawa prefecture and part of Kagoshima prefecture – was a country with a monarchy and its own territory, language, culture, and diplomatic relations. However, the Ryukyu Kingdom as an 'other' country in Japan ended after the annexation of the Ryukyus in 1879, when Okinawa was completely incorporated into the Japanese state (Takara 1988: 27). From that period to the present day, the history of Okinawa has been distorted in Japan, especially in school education, which is an important basis for Japanese people's historical perceptions. For example, Shibutani and Iwamoto (2014) state that the history of the Ryukyu Kingdom is not emphasized in the Japanese curriculum. Any mention of the Ryukyu Kingdom in textbooks appears only in sections regarding Satsuma's invasion of Ryukyu (1609) and the Ryukyu Disposition (1879), while the kingdom's relationship with Japan before or between these events is treated with ambiguity. They cite results of questionnaire surveys revealing that many Japanese students thought that Okinawa was part of Japan all along, and some students even thought that the Ryukyu Kingdom had done something bad because of the word *shobun* ('disposition' in the context of the 'Ryukyu Disposition', but *shobun* can also mean 'punishment') (Shibutani and Iwamoto 2014: 47). By contrast, the Battle of Okinawa (1945) at the end of the Second World War is strongly

DOI: 10.4324/9781003239970-8

emphasized in Japanese textbooks. As Takara notes, it is important to convey Second World War history, but it is just one part of the history of Ryukyu/Okinawa (Takara 1993: 8–10).

The major Japanese work of popular culture depicting the Satsuma domain's invasion of the Ryukyu Kingdom in 1609 from a Ryukyuan perspective is *Ryukyu no Kaze: Dragon Spirit* (1993).[1] The drama is based on a novel of the same title (written specifically to be the basis of the drama) by Chinese–Japanese author Chin Shunshin (Haraguchi 2018: 53). The drama is set in the Ryukyu Kingdom in the first half of the seventeenth century. It tells how the protagonists try to gain independence for their kingdom as a trading country between Japan and China despite the Satsuma invasion. While many Taiga dramas have real historical figures as the main characters, in *Ryukyu no Kaze* the main character Keitai is fictional. Keitai was born on a ship going from Ryukyu to Ming China and spent his childhood in China before being separated from his parents when pirates attacked his home. He and his brother moved to Ryukyu. After many twists and turns, it is revealed that his father was working as a doctor for the Shimazu family, the lords of Satsuma and instigators of the Ryukyu invasion. Through the life story of a fictional character, the situation in Ryukyu at that time is dramatically portrayed. The drama was especially popular in Okinawa, although the use of Japanese actors to play Ryukyuans, the lack of local dialect, and the 'mediated "Yamatoization (Yamatoka, i.e., Japanization)" of Okinawa-as-Ryukyu designed for mainland Japanese consumption' generated considerable criticism, too (Figal 2012: 163–164). However, this Yamatoization might have been out of ignorance rather than design. As mentioned previously by Takara, there is often a lack of basic understanding regarding Okinawa in Japan. Furthermore, the original author, Chin, was not recognized as a well-versed authority on Ryukyu history and culture (Haraguchi 2018: 53). Partly in response to such concerns, in 1994 (the year after the initial broadcast) a version dubbed in the Ryukyuan language was aired again in Okinawa.

Ryukyu no Kaze contributed to the revitalization of tourism in Okinawa. In 1992, a year before the drama aired and the 20th year after Okinawa's return to Japan from the United States, Shuri Castle, which had been destroyed in the Pacific War in 1945, was restored (Benesch and Zwigenberg 2019). The restored Shuri Castle (Figure 6.1) was widely used in the drama, including a scene depicting the visit of an emissary from the Ming Dynasty in 1606. The filming set for the drama was made in Yomitan village, Okinawa prefecture, and opened to tourists as the Studio Park Nankai Kingdom Ryukyu no Kaze after the shooting. At the end of each episode, the drama introduced places related to the story

Figure 6.1 Shuri Castle. This picture was taken before it burnt down in 2019. Photo:
     Yamamura Takayoshi.

(this is a feature of Taiga dramas, and partly explains their power as tourism drivers). In *Ryukyu no Kaze*, the title of the corner was *Churaumi kikō*, which means beautiful sea travel (Figal 2012: 159).

The drama conveyed the exotic topography, scenery, and culture of Ryukyu. Okinawa received a boost as a tourist destination, not only because of the various sites connected with the filming but also because the collapse of the bubble economy caused many Japanese people to favour domestic over international tourism. Products to stimulate tourism consumption were also developed. The release of awamori (traditional Okinawan liquor) called 'Churaumi travel' (Ishigaki 1995), named after the section at the end of the drama, and 'Keitai', named after the main character, contributed to increasing tourism revenue and promoting the Okinawa brand throughout the country.

The revitalization of tourism through the drama combined the existing exotic image of Okinawa with the image of the Ryukyu Kingdom, resulting in what Gerald Figal refers to as 'Tropical Kingdom Okinawa' (Figal 2012: 165). Associated tourism campaigns had little incentive to focus on the historical facts of Satsuma's invasion of Ryukyu.

For example, a tourism campaign conducted by Japanese airline ANA focused on tropical images of the Ryukyu Kingdom, while the description of the Ryukyus evoked the Okinawa and Ryukyu spirit (Figal 2012: 166). Also, this overlap was not highlighted after *Ryukyu no Kaze*. There has not been a terrestrial TV drama of similar stature dealing with the relationship between the Ryukyu Kingdom and Japan since *Ryukyu no Kaze*. NHK's dramas centred on Okinawa typically emphasize Okinawa's image as an island paradise in the modern world.

However, as with every other instance of Taiga drama tourism, there was a decline in the number of tourists from the year after the drama aired. Visitors to the studio park, who numbered about 520,000 in the year the drama aired, declined sharply from 1994. By the end of the 1990s, the facility was operating at a loss and attracting only 100,000 people a year (Asahi Shinbun 1999). The studio park went bankrupt and closed in March 1999. It was transferred to Yomitan village and since 2000 it has been operated under the name Experience Kingdom Murasaki Mura by a new company established by members of the municipal Chamber of Commerce and Industry. The financial difficulties of this site were a salient lesson for tourism operators across Japan about the risks of developing large sites of contents tourism on the back of the Taiga drama. These days, any sets and attractions linked to the drama tend to be open only in the year the drama is aired.

In summary, *Ryukyu no Kaze* is conspicuous for being one of only a few dramas about the history of the Ryukyu Kingdom from a Ryukyuan perspective. While there were clear, temporary tourism effects because of the drama around the time of the broadcast, and while the drama was partly successful in remaking the image of the Ryukyu Kingdom, it has not generated a decisive shift in terms of historical consciousness. The history of the invasion and colonization of the Ryukyu Kingdom remains side-lined and relatively unknown in Japan. War and tourism in Okinawa remain connected more strongly to memories of the Second World War, after Okinawa was incorporated into Japan, rather than by the seventeenth-century invasion that paved the way for Okinawa to become part of Japan in the first place.

Note

1   Another drama is *Tempest* (2011), which aired on the NHK satellite channel.

References

Asahi Shinbun, 1999. Tēmapāku 'Ryūkyū no kaze' sonzoku e shōkōkai ni itaku Okinawa. *Asahi Shinbun* [seibu], 30 March, p. 30.

Benesch, O. and Zwigenberg, R., 2019. Shuri castle and Japanese castles: a controversial heritage. *The Asia-Pacific Journal: Japan Focus*, 17 (24), 3. https://apjjf.org/2019/24/Benesch.

Figal, G., 2012. *Beachheads: war, peace, and tourism in postwar Okinawa*. Lanham: Rowman & Littlefield.

Haraguchi, I., 2018. Saigō Takamori to bungaku. *Kinsei bungei*, 108, 53–66.

Ishigaki, S., 1995. Awamori koshu 'konpeki' shirīzu no kaihatsu. *Nihon jōzō kyōkai-shi*, 90, 499–503.

Sasaki, T., 2011. Hitotsu no rettō, futatsu no kokka, mittsu no bunka. *Gakujutsu no dōkō*, 16 (9), 70–78.

Shibutani, T. and Iwamoto, H., 2014. Shōgakkō shakai-ka rekishi gakushū ni okeru 'Ryūkyū ōkoku' no tangen kaihatsu. *Kyōiku jissen kaihatsu kenkyū sentā kenkyū kiyō*, 23, 41–48.

Takara, K., 1988. Ryūkyū Okinawa to nihonshi-zō, *Rekishigaku kenkyū*, 586, 22–30.

Takara, K., 1993. *Ryukyu ōkoku*. Tokyo: Iwanami Shoten.

7 War-related narratives and contents tourism during the 'Tokugawa peace'

Takayoshi Yamamura

Matsuo Basho (1644–1694) is one of the most famous *haiku* (Japanese 17-syllable poem) poets of the early Edo era. Modern domestic Japanese tourists and international tourists continue to visit the places where Basho wrote his *haiku* (Beeton 2020).

The following is one of his war-related *haiku*:

> The summer grasses —
> Of brave soldiers' dreams
> The aftermath.
>
> (Matsuo 2007: 125)

It appears in the chapter *Hiraizumi* in his travel writing masterpiece *Oku no Hosomichi* (*The Narrow Road to the Interior*). The chapter containing this *haiku* depicts the deep emotion that Basho felt when visiting a historical battle site.

War-related contents tourism in the early Edo period can be understood from the preamble to the *haiku*.

> It was at Palace-on-the-Heights that Yoshitsune and his picked retainers fortified themselves, but his glory turned in a moment into this wilderness of grass. 'Countries may fall, but their rivers and mountains remain; when spring comes to the ruined castle, the grass is green again'. These lines went through my head as I sat on the ground, my bamboo hat spread under me. There I sat weeping, unaware of the passage of time.
>
> (Matsuo 2007: 125–126)

Basho was visiting Takadachi (Koromogawa-no-tachi), the former residence of the warlord Minamoto no Yoshitsune (1159–1189). He felt that he had travelled back in time to when Yoshitsune died at this place.

DOI: 10.4324/9781003239970-9

The tragic warrior Yoshitsune, 'despite his many exploits in battle, was treated with hostility and tracked down by his elder brother Yoritomo' (Inumaru 2014: 42). In 1189, he was reportedly attacked by the soldiers of Fujiwara no Yasuhira, who had sided with Yoritomo at Hiraizumi. Despite his loyal subjects' efforts, Yoshitsune was forced to commit suicide (Kadokawa Shoten 2001: 115–116).

While few accurate records of Yoshitsune remain (Yabumoto 2011: 1), the book *Gikei-ki* (*Military Epic about the Life of Yoshitsune*, author unknown), appeared in the early Muromachi era (around the fourteenth century) (Sato and Kobayashi 1968: 274). It dramatically depicts the end of Yoshitsune's life at Hiraizumi. Therefore, one can reasonably assume that in Hiraizumi Basho saw 'the remains of a battle, as narrated in *Gikei-ki*' (Nakagawa 1997: 11). Moreover, *The Narrow Road to the Interior* features the following *haiku* by Kawai Sora, a disciple who accompanied Basho on his travels.

In the verbena
I seem to see Kanefusa —
Behold his white hair!   (Sora)

(Matsuo 2007: 125)

'Kanefusa' is Jurogon-no-kami Kanefusa, a character in *Gikei-ki* (Takagi 2004: 646), who is not mentioned in the historical record. This suggests that Basho and his disciple Sora were reliving *Gikei-ki*'s narrative world, which was based on historical facts, albeit containing a strong fictional element.

Gunki-monogatari and its popularisation in the Edo era

Japanese literary works based on historical battles (for example, *Gikei-ki*) are called *gunki-monogatari* or *gunki-mono* (military epics or war chronicles). This literary genre was reportedly established between the Kamakura era (twelfth to fourteenth centuries) and Muromachi era (fourteenth to sixteenth centuries) (Takahashi 2015: 677). *Heike monogatari* (*The Tale of the Heike*) exemplifies the genre in this period (Kusaka 2008: i–ii). The *gunki-monogatari* genre developed greatly during the Edo period (seventeenth to nineteenth centuries). After the Warring States period (fifteenth to sixteenth centuries) ended, many *gunki-monogatari* were published and gained a large readership (Takahashi 2015: 677).

During the Tokugawa peace or 'Pax Tokugawa' (Okuno 2007: 102), which lasted for about 250 years, Japanese popular culture and entertainment flourished in two aspects: the popularisation of tourism (Kanzaki

2004: 237) and the rise and diversification of entertainment industries, including kabuki, sumo, and *yose* comedy (Ando 2009: 58). The foundations of modern Japanese popular entertainment were formed during this period. Basho's war-related contents tourism can be understood within this context. In short, war-related contents tourism was popularized and matured during the Edo era, both in terms of contents and tourism.

Yoshitsune's legendary journey to Hokkaido and Mongolia

Gikei-ki became the source of a large number of classical works, including noh theatre, ningyō-jōruri (Japanese puppetry), and kabuki (Tsuji 2017: 84). Kabuki plays such as *Yoshitsune senbonzakura* (*Yoshitsune and One Thousand Cherry Trees*, first performed in 1748) and *Kangjincho* (*A Subscription Book*, first performed in 1840) are typical examples of *Gikei-ki* adaptations (Inumaru 2014: 32–43). As these kabuki plays received many performances, Yoshitsune's popularity grew, especially in Edo (present-day Tokyo). In particular, Yoshitsune's 'tragic life', as depicted in *Kanjincho*, 'was overwhelmingly sympathized with by the common people of Edo' (Inumaru 2014: 42). As Kanzaki also points out, tourism had become popular among ordinary people throughout Japan by the mid-Edo period, and kabuki performances became regular events outside Edo, too (Kanzaki 2004: 100).

In this way, the narrative world of Yoshitsune, which mixed fiction and reality, captured the hearts of ordinary Japanese people and 'the image of a legendary hero was formed'. 'A story was created that Yoshitsune's suicide at Hiraizumi was faked, he escaped from Japan alive, and crossed from Ezo (Hokkaido) to the continent' (Fukuta *et al.* 1999: 776). Many sites connected to the legendary narrative of Yoshitsune's escape are still found in Hokkaido and Tohoku (northern Honshu), and they continue to attract many tourists (Figure 7.1).

Matsuura Takeshiro (1818–1888) was an explorer who surveyed Ezo-chi (modern-day Hokkaido) and invented the name 'Hokkaido'. He left many detailed written records of his surveys, and in his journals he recorded a number of Yoshitsune legends from around Hokkaido. For example, the book *Ezo kunmo zui* (circa 1860) contains the following explanatory text and a drawing of Yoshitsune and his loyal subject Benkei.

> Once upon a time, Yoshitsune, Benkei and many other samurai came to this island in ships ... Then, they entered Karafuto (Sakhalin)

Figure 7.1 Kamuy Rock, Shakotan, Hokkaido. The monolith on the small island in the centre is one of the places where the legend of Yoshitsune's journey to the north survives. According to local legend, Charenka, an Ainu lady who adored Yoshitsune, threw herself into the sea in despair and became a rock when she heard that Yoshitsune had left for the continent. Author's photo.

Island, hoping that the countries to the north of Hokkaido would be controlled by Japan.

(Matsuura 1997: 80–81)

Moreover, in his book *Nishi-Ezo nisshi* (*Journal of West Hokkaido* [circa 1860]), he introduced the theory, advocated by Philipp Franz Balthasar von Siebold (a German doctor residing in Japan at the time) that Yoshitsune 'left Ezo (Hokkaido), crossed to Northeast China, went to Mongolia ...', and ascended to the imperial throne', becoming 'the original founder Genghis Khan' (Matsuura 1984: 64–65). Current historiography and archaeology do not support these narratives, and they are considered to be merely products of the imagination. However, such narratives were circulating widely among the public, including the intelligentsia, at a time (mid-nineteenth century) when Japan needed to demarcate its northern borders, especially those with Russia. This is one reason why Japan was particularly keen to incorporate Hokkaido into Japan.

The modern Japanese public continues to consume pop culture and generate tourism related to the narrative world of Yoshitsune, which has been repeatedly re-edited within a mixed context of reality and fiction. It has expanded into an almost fictional epic of heroism travelling across national borders. Several local governments or DMOs (Destination Management/Marketing Organizations) in Tohoku and Hokkaido, which are located further north than Hiraizumi (Iwate prefecture, where Yoshitsune is said to have died) are promoting places associated with the legend of Yoshitsune's journey to the north as tourist attractions today (for example, Visit Hachinohe 2019).

Conclusion

This chapter has discussed how the *gunki-monogatari* genre was established during the Kamakura era and matured as a form of popular culture during the Edo era, which saw the growth of war-related contents tourism practices. The narrative world of Yoshitsune is a typical example of this development. It has been re-edited for over 800 years; furthermore, it was already inducing contents tourism almost 400 years ago. By tracing the adaptation processes of the contents and the tourism induced by *gunki-monogatari* as an early form of war-related contents tourism (both in terms of contents and tourism), discussion becomes possible regarding contents tourism from a historical and sociocultural perspective. It also becomes possible to consider the intersections of heritage and contents tourism studies, rather than seeing contents tourism simply as a theory relevant only to contemporary popular culture or media-induced phenomena.

References

Ando, Y., 2009. *Goraku-toshi Edo no yūwaku*. Tokyo: PHP Kenkyujo.

Beeton, S., 2020. From Banjo to Basho: poets, contents and tourism. *In*: T. Yamamura and P. Seaton, eds. *Contents tourism and pop culture fandom: transnational tourist experiences*. Bristol: Channel View Publications, 205–223.

Fukuta, A., Kanda, Y., Shintani, T., Nakagomi, M., Yukawa, Y. and Watanabe, Y., eds, 1999. *Nihon minzoku daijiten (jō)*. Tokyo: Yoshikawa kōbunkan.

Inumaru, O., 2014. *Kabuki nyūmon*. Tokyo: Sekaibunkasha.

Kadokawa Shoten, ed., 2001. *Beginner's classics Oku no hosomichi (zen)*. Tokyo: Kadokawa Bunko.

Kanzaki, N., 2004. *Edo no tabi-bunka*. Tokyo: Iwanami Shoten.

Kusaka, T., 2008. *Ikusa monogatari no sekai: chūsē gunki-bungaku wo yomu*. Tokyo: Iwanami Shoten.

Matsuo, B. (trans. D. Keene), 2007. *Oku no hosomichi/The narrow road to Oku*. Tokyo: Kodansha.

Matsuura, T., 1984. *Shinban Ezo nisshi (ge)*. Tokyo: Jijitsushinsha.

Matsuura, T., 1997. *Matsuura Takeshiro senshū vol.2*. Sapporo: Hokkaido Shuppan Kikaku Centre.

Nakagawa, M., 1997. Study on haiku in the 'Narrow road to a far province'. *Research Review of Education and Research Center for Lifelong Learning*, Kagawa University 2, 1–23.

Okuno, T., 2007. *Japan cool to Edo bunka*. Tokyo: Iwanami Shoten.

Sato, K. and Kobayashi, K., 1968. *Gikei-ki 1*. Tokyo: Heibonsha.

Takagi, T., 2004. *Gendaigo-yaku Gikei-ki*. Tokyo: Kawade Shobo Shinsha.

Takahashi, K., 2015. Gunki, senki. *In*: N. Kanzaki, Y. Shirahata, and S. Inoue, eds. *Nihon bunka jiten*. Tokyo: Maruzen Shuppan, 676–677.

Tsuji, K., 2017. *Kabuki no kaibō-zukan*. Tokyo: Xknowledge.

Visit Hachinohe, 2019. *Hachinohe shinai ni nokoru 'Yoshitsune hokkō densetsu'*. Visit Hachinohe. https://visithachinohe.com/stories/yoshitsune/.

Yabumoto, K., 2011. *Gikei-ki no kenkyū*. Doctoral dissertation (Doctor of Literature), Kobe University.

8 Tōken Ranbu and samurai swords as tourist attractions

Akiko Sugawa-Shimada

Japanese swords (*nihontō*) are generally regarded as weapons for samurai warriors, but they have various symbolic and aesthetic values in Japanese culture. In *Kojiki* (*Records of Ancient Matters*) and *Nihonshoki* (*Chronicles of Japan*) in the eighth century, it was said that a sword was one of the Three Sacred Treasures of Japanese imperial regalia that Ninigi, a grandson of Amaterasu the Sun Goddess, brought to the ground from Takamagahara heavens. Based on this myth, swords became objects of worship in Shinto. Additionally, in Japanese Buddhist and Shinto belief, a sword protects its owner from demons, so it is regarded as a talisman (Sugawa-Shimada 2020a: 59). In the Heian period (794–1185), a sword was a treasure bestowed by the emperor, and it was gifted to noblemen for their great achievement in the court (Kawashima 2020: n.p.). Following this tradition, after the Kamakura period feudal loads (*daimyō*) also gave *nihontō* to samurai for meritorious service.

From the Kamakura period (1185–1333) to the Warring States period (late sixteenth century), swords were not used in battle as often as other weapons, such as spears, bows, and arrows (Watabe 2021: 2; Kawashima 2020: n.p.). However, during the Tokugawa period (1603–1868), when class distinctions were solidified, only the samurai class was allowed to carry a pair of long and short *nihontō*. Swords symbolized samurai status, and this image has been reproduced in popular culture. After the Haitōrei (law prohibiting the carrying of swords) of 1876, intellectuals such as Nitobe Inazō (author of *Bushidō: The Soul of Japan*) in the Meiji period (1868–1912) used swords' symbolic value to construct a national identity associated with *bushidō* (way of the samurai). In the 1930s, during the Second Sino-Japanese War, the symbolic value of *nihontō* was enhanced again. Japanese soldiers wore *nihontō* to symbolize loyalty and masculinity in reference to samurai (Watabe 2021: 3). After the Second World War, the 1958 Act for Controlling the Possession of Firearms or Swords and Other Such Weapons was enacted. Swords were defined as

DOI: 10.4324/9781003239970-10

artefacts and their images as weapons sanitized. In recent times, therefore, *nihontō* in Japanese culture have been seen as works of art, but historically they have also been weapons of war and ritual tools in Shinto and Japanese Buddhism. Overall, swords frequently invoke a national sensibility (Watabe 2021).

Young people used to pay little attention to *nihontō* as works of art. But they suddenly gained popularity, especially among young women, due to the online game *Tōken Ranbu-ONLINE-* (2015–present) and its transmedia franchise. *Tōken Ranbu* (literally 'boisterous dance of swords') is a DMM and Nitroplus action game played on web browsers and apps. It features handsome young men called *Tōken danshi* (sword male warriors), who are the 'artifact spirits' (*tsukumogami*) of Japanese swords modelled on actual swords of historically famous figures from the twelfth to the nineteenth centuries.[1] Gamers play the role of a *saniwa* (shaman-like person) who has magical power to ensoul swords. The game has no specific storyline but the 'world' (*sekaikan*) is set in 2205 when historical revisionists attempt to change Japanese history by sending their demon-like army to the past. To prevent their plot, the government orders a *saniwa* to maintain 'history' by sending *Tōken danshi* to the past.

Tōken Ranbu-ONLINE- was adapted into musicals (2015–present), plays (2016–present), a live action film (2019), two TV anime series (*Tōken Ranbu: Hanamaru*, 2016 and 2018; *Katsugeki! Tōken Ranbu*, 2017), and Internet radio programmes. Collaborations with tourist sites vary from Tōken saryou (2016–2019), a café in Akihabara with real *nihontō* displayed in glass showcases, to sword exhibitions in museums. The musicals and play series are some of the most popular works among young women and have induced theatre tourism as a form of contents tourism (Sugawa-Shimada 2020b: 135; Chapter 14). A special live concert from the musical *Tōken Ranbu* was held at Itsukushima Shrine in Hiroshima in 2016 to celebrate the twentieth anniversary of it becoming a World Heritage Site. In Shinto, *kagura* (traditional Shinto dance) and *gagaku* music are routinely performed as a sacred ritual for *kami* (Shinto gods). Thus, dance and songs by *Tōken danshi* (personified swords) at a world heritage Shinto shrine had the potential to stimulate a sense of spirituality and national sensitivity, although most female fans who attended the concert in Itsukushima Shrine concentrated on the characters/actors and seemed to pay no attention to the symbolic and negative meanings that *nihontō* can have (Sugawa-Shimada 2020a: 62).

During the *nihontō* boom induced by *Tōken Ranbu*, a number of museums all over Japan put on displays of swords related to the game, and female fans sometimes called *Tōken joshi* in the media flooded to them (The Mainichi 2020). The five-minute TV series *Tōken Ranbu, okkii*

Konnosuke no Tōken sanpo (*Tōken Ranbu,* big Konnosuke's sword walking tour, broadcast 2017–2019 on Tokyo MX TV) introduced swords on display in museums and shrines in Japan, which also facilitated female fans' contents tourism (Figure 8.1).

Even museums whose exhibitions did not collaborate with *Tōken Ranbu* have seen an increase in visitors: for instance, the Hijikata Toshizō Museum in Hino city, Tokyo, which displays Izumi no kami Kanesada, the long sword of Hijikata Toshizō; and the Satō Hikogorō Shinsengumi Museum in Hino, which displays Hijikata's photo, swords, and letters (Chapter 10). A female fan who I talked to at the Hijikata Toshizō Museum in 2019 told me that she was 'so happy to meet' (*aete, mecha ureshii*) Izumi no kami Kanesada (a character of *Tōken Ranbu*). She came all the way from the Kansai area to see 'him'.

In other notable cases of *Tōken Ranbu*-related contents tourism, fans have contributed to the rediscovery or restoration of *nihontō* as Japanese art or to the broader disaster recovery effort after the Kumamoto Earthquake of 2016 and the 2020 Kyushu floods.

In actual history, Shokudaigiri Mitsutada, a sword of Date Masamune (a famous *daimyō* in the Warring States period), was handed down to the

Figure 8.1 *Tōken Ranbu* fans looking at other fans' *ema* (votive wooden tablets), Kaji Shrine, Kyoto. Author's photo.

Mito Tokugawa Family, but it was thought to have been destroyed in the Great Kanto Earthquake in 1923. Although its whereabouts were unknown to sword fans, after Mitsutada appeared as a *Tōken danshi* in the game, the Tokugawa Museum in Mito city announced that it was stored at the museum, but was too heavily damaged by fire to be displayed as an artwork. However, following fans' requests, the Tokugawa Museum has held special exhibits since 2015 and become one of the most popular destinations for fans ever since (Mikame 2018). There is a similar story about Hotarumaru, a *Tōken danshi* modelled on the large sword Hotarumaru Kunitoshi, which was lost during the Second World War. Swordsmith Fukutome Fusayuki started a crowdfunding project called Hotarumaru Legend Recovery Project in 2015.[2] It exceeded its target and raised around 45 million yen, which was probably supported heavily by fans (Kumamoto Kenmin TV 2017). A newly forged Hotarumaru was dedicated to Aso Shrine in 2017.

The Hotarumaru Legend Recovery Project also contributed to the recovery of Aso Shrine, which was almost destroyed in the Kumamoto Earthquake of 2016. *Tōken joshi* also contributed to disaster recovery efforts at Aoi Aso Shrine in Hitoyoshi city, Kumamoto. The 77 swords dedicated to this shrine were submerged in the 2020 Kyushu floods. Although these swords were not directly related to *Tōken Ranbu* characters, 'many female fans of *Tōken Ranbu* ... supported the crowdfunding to rescue 77 swords dedicated to Aoi Aso Shrine' (Hitoyoshi Shinbun 2020). Fans donated to this project because they are not only fans of the game. As sword fans they wanted to help any sword damaged by natural disaster.

In summary, Japanese swords (*nihontō*) have symbolic and aesthetic value in Japanese culture. The transmedia franchise *Tōken Ranbu* deftly sanitizes their negative images related to wars and has popularized them using handsome young male characters modelled on the actual swords of historically famous figures. Paying little attention to such war-related connotations that *nihontō* can convey, fans, many of whom are female (*Tōken joshi*), enthusiastically visit shrines, museums, birth and death places of historical figures who were the models for their favourite sword characters, and other related sites nationwide. However, the nationalistic samurai spirits connected to swords unexpectedly appeared when Chinese and Korean fans of *Tōken Ranbu* harshly condemned a 2017 stamp rally called 'Cherry blossom tour in Edo castle district' in Tokyo done in collaboration with *Tōken Ranbu* that had Yasukuni Shrine as one of the stops (Togetter 2017; Chapter 15). Yasukuni Shrine is often criticized because it enshrines war criminals. Japanese swords are double-edged indeed.

Notes

1 The director of *Tōken Ranbu* intentionally avoided using swords from the twentieth century as game characters because they are strongly connected to killing in wars (Watabe 2021: 15).
2 The legend of Hotarumaru: The large sword of Aso Korezumi was damaged during battle against Ashikaga Takauji in 1336. It is said that the blade of Aso's sword was restored after he dreamed that countless fireflies were perched on it. Based on this legend, this sword was called Hotarumaru (the fireflies) and was later dedicated to Aso Shrine (Kumamoto Kenmin TV 2017).

References

Hitoyoshi Shinbun, 2020. Sabita suibotsu hōnōtō 77 furi, shufuku e josei fanra shien hirogaru. *Hitoyoshi Shinbun*, 27 August. https://hitoyoshi-sharepla.com/entrance _news.php?news=3790.

Kawashima, T., 2020. *Nihontō to nihonjin*. Tokyo: Gentōsha. [Kindle]

Kumamoto Kenmin TV, 2017. *Hotarumaru o fukugen seyo!* Kumamoto Kenmin TV. https://www.kkt.jp/matome/hotarumaru/.

The Mainichi, 2020. Huge demand from Japan 'sword girls' drives sales of $350 blade-themed photo book. *The Mainichi*, 1 March. https://mainichi.jp/english/ articles/20200228/p2a/00m/0et/011000c.

Mikame, Y., 2018. *'Token Ranbu-ONLINE' de chūmoku sareta katana 'Shokudaigiri Mitsutada' no kagayaki ga yomigaeru made wo Tokugawa Museum ni kiku.* https:// news.denfaminicogamer.jp/interview/180720/amp.

Sugawa-Shimada, A., 2020a. Animating artifact spirits in the 2.5-dimensional world: personification and performing characters in *Token Ranbu*. *In*: G. Hu, M. Yokota, and G. Horvath, eds. *Animating the spirited: journeys and transformations*. Jackson: University Press of Mississippi, 55–65.

Sugawa-Shimada, A., 2020b. The 2.5-dimensional theatre as a communication site: non-site-specific theatre tourism. *In*: T. Yamamura and P. Seaton, eds. *Contents tourism and pop culture fandom: transnational tourist experiences*. Bristol: Channel View Publications, 128–143.

Togetter, 2017. Enjō, Tōken Ranbu-Online- no Yasukuni jinja korabo ni chūkan yūzā kara hihan sattōàichibu henkō e. *Togetter*, 10 March. https://togetter.com/ li/1088979.

Watabe, K., 2021. Japanese swords as symbols of historical amnesia: Touken ranbu and the sword boom in popular media. *The Asia-Pacific Journal: Japan Focus*, 19 (7), 1. https://apjjf.org/2021/7/Watabe.html.

9 Castles and castle towns in Japanese tourism

Yosuke Fujiki and Hitoshi Nakai

A deep water-filled moat, high stone walls, and a castle keep on top of the stone walls − but above all, the keep is the symbol of a castle, and the place that we imagine became a stronghold during battles and where warlords and their vassals gathered. This is probably the common image of Japanese castles in the Warring States period (1467–1590, hereafter Sengoku period). However, most such images of castles are formed by television dramas and films and are entirely fictional.

For example, in the film *Kagemusha* (1980) directed by Kurosawa Akira, the stone walls and keep of Kumamoto Castle (Figure 9.1) were shown in the scene where the warlord Takeda Shingen (1521–1573) attacks Noda Castle, and the stone walls and keep of Himeji Castle were used as the residence of the warlord Oda Nobunaga (1534–1582). Hikone Castle and Iga Ueno Castle were also used as filming locations.

However, none of the castles used in *Kagemusha* date from the Sengoku period. The same issue existed in Chapter 4 − *Sekiro: Shadows Die Twice*, which featured a castle from a later period than when the game was supposedly set. In reality, Sengoku period castles were very different to the castles used in the film and game. Stone walls and keeps only became part of general castle design from the Azuchi-Momoyama period (1573–1603), when warfare in various parts of the country was subsiding. There were no keeps in the castles of the Sengoku period, and stone walls were found in only a few castles. Keeps were built from the Early Modern period (1573–1868) and therefore played little to no role in actual wars. Today, there are 12 original keeps that have survived from the time when they were built. None of them was used in actual wars, although the survival of these original castles to the present inevitably incorporates a narrative of how they were spared destruction not only in the period of castle demolition after the Meiji Restoration (1868) but during the air raids of 1944–1945 (Benesch and Zwigenberg 2019).

DOI: 10.4324/9781003239970-11

Figure 9.1 Kumamoto Castle. Author's photo.

Furthermore, the feudal lords who ruled the surrounding territory rarely entered the keeps.

Despite such historical inaccuracies, castle tourism has become increasingly popular in recent years, bolstered by the image of castles in popular culture. When we climb the keeps as castle tourists, we can look out over the surrounding area and feel like a Sengoku period warlord, even though the lords did not actually see such a landscape. Castle tourism playing on the imagination and tourism imaginaries can be fun, and it is not necessarily bad to enjoy fictional images like this. But this chapter demonstrates the more authentic way of enjoying castle tourism, namely via knowledge of the meaning of the original castle.

Sengoku and Early Modern castles

Broadly speaking, castles began as moated settlements built by villages during the Yayoi period (third century BC to third century AD). A castle can be defined as 'a facility to protect certain areas under the control of a group of people from enemies'.

In the period of the Northern and Southern Courts (1337–1392), war broke out across the whole country. Many forts were built on steep mountains as defensive positions and used the natural terrain to their advantage. They were called *yamajiro*, 'mountain castles', and built specifically to fight wars. From the Northern and Southern Courts period to the middle of the Sengoku period, when warfare was fierce nationwide, all castles were *yamajiro*. During the Sengoku period, the technology for building *yamajiro* developed significantly. They were built with *dorui*, walls of heaped soil, and *horikiri*, ditches cut out of the soil. There were no buildings such as keeps in *yamajiro,* and only simple huts and turrets to observe enemy movements.

Yamajiro were fortifications to protect the surrounding area, but people stayed there only during wars. In peacetime, people lived in *kyo-kan*, residences at the foot of the mountain. *Yamajiro* were never used as residences. In the latter half of the Sengoku period, *yamajiro* became larger. Sometimes stone walls were built and residences where people lived during wartime were built on the mountains. However, the design of *yamajiro* as fortifications remained, and keeps were never built. The remains of *yamajiro* fortifications can still be seen in various places around Japan, although there are no surviving *yamajiro* buildings.

Then Azuchi Castle was built by Oda Nobunaga in 1576–1579. This was the first castle in which a keep was combined with stone walls. Its luxurious tall keep was decorated with gold leaf tiles. It became the prototype for castles in the Early Modern period. Nobunaga had asserted his control over the warlords in the Kinai area of central Japan and presided over a certain level of peace. Nobunaga used the castle as a means of demonstrating his power to the people and other feudal lords. It is said that Nobunaga lived in the keep and looked out over his realm. Thereafter, while maintaining its defensive function the castle became a symbol of power with an element of being 'for show'. Toyotomi Hideyoshi (1537–1598) and other warlords followed suit, building castles with large keeps to demonstrate their power. However, warlords usually lived in a residence called a *goten* in the castle compound. It was separate from the keep and lords never lived in the keep itself. Most warlords did not even go up to the keep. Nobunaga was the only warlord who lived in the keep, either before or after his death (Nakai and Saitō 2016).

Early Modern castles and castle towns

In the Edo period (1603–1868), the Tokugawa shogunate ordered the *daimyo* (feudal lords) of various domains to carry out civil engineering and construction work. Castles were built under this *tenkabushin* policy at strategic points in each region. These are the castles with keeps at various places around Japan today. For example, Hikone Castle (completed in

1622) was at a strategic point connecting the Kinki district and the Tokai district to protect the shogunate from the Toyotomi clan in Osaka. It was built under the *tenkabushin* policy. Construction was started by Ii Naotsugu (1590–1662) in 1603. It is one of the five castles whose keep is designated as a national treasure (the others are Inuyama Castle, Matsumoto Castle, Himeji Castle, and Matsue Castle). Hikone Castle is famous for its *nobori-ishigaki* (vertical stone walls to prevent attackers from moving around the slopes up to the keep). *Nobori-ishigaki* are rare in Japan and required considerable engineering expertise to construct.

After the Tokugawa clan defeated the Toyotomi clan in the Battle of Osaka (summer 1614 and winter 1615 campaigns), the Edo period was a peaceful era without major warfare (Chapter 7). This changed the role of the castle as a military facility. In Sengoku period castles, the fortifications (*yamajiro*) and residences (*kyokan*) were in different places. However, in the Early Modern castles, it was common for the daimyo's residence (*goten*) to be built inside the castle. Castles were visited by vassals and played a central role in the politics of the land. Residential areas grew in the areas around the castles. Vassals and common people lived in castle towns (*jōkamachi*), which grew into Japan's major cities today (Nakai and Kamiyu Rekishi Henshūbu 2018).

The main function of the castle was as the political centre of the city, but it was still a military base, too. The keep was almost useless militarily. However, keeps were still built more luxuriously than other buildings in the castle. Even in peaceful times, the keep was indispensable 'for show' as a symbol of power. Walking up to Hikone Castle, the keep looks unexpectedly small because the width of the keep is narrower when seen from the path up to it. The façade facing the town is wider and looks dignified when viewed from the town. The sides not visible from the town were narrowed to reduce construction costs. This demonstrates that the keep was built specifically 'for show'. They are now familiar to people as symbols of their respective cities. Indeed, many of Japan's castles today – including those in Hiroshima, Osaka, Okayama, and others – are modern reconstructions built to recreate a historical landmark and to attract tourists (Benesch and Zwigenberg 2019).

Castles and (war-related contents) tourism

Sengoku period castles were fortifications designed for defence. In the mountainous regions of Japan, you can still find many remains of *yamajiro* from the Sengoku period. They use subtle engineering of the terrain and are essentially remodelled mountain tops. The best way to enjoy Sengoku castle tourism is through appreciation of the engineering of the terrain while imagining the actual wars fought at these places. By contrast, the surviving original castles from the Early Modern period exist to this day precisely because they did not experience destruction or significant damage in war. Rather they were centres of regional politics. However, the cityscapes of Japan's modern cities are centred on these castles. These cityscapes are not only familiar to local people, but also attract tourists, including contents tourists who have seen these castles used as locations in films and television dramas.

Given their historical roles, Japan's surviving castles present an irony. They were buildings constructed to project the power and self-esteem of the castle owners and were not particularly necessary for war. Some castles with keeps did see fighting – most notably Osaka Castle (1614–1615), sites of Boshin War battles (1868–1869, Aizu-Wakamatsu, Nagaoka, Matsumae), and Kumamoto Castle during the Satsuma Rebellion (1877) – and others were destroyed during the air raids on Japan in 1944–1945. But, for the most part, Japan's keep castles can hardly be seen as sites of war-related tourism because wars were not fought there. However, through the imagination of them as sites of battles among samurai created by historical films/dramas/games and their use as locations for other historical dramas (like *Clouds Above the Hill* – Chapter 12) and even James Bond (Himeji Castle was a shooting location for *You Only Live Twice*), castles are often important sites of war-related contents tourism.

References

Benesch, O. and Zwigenberg, R., 2019. *Japan's castles: citadels of modernity in war and peace*. Cambridge: Cambridge University Press.

Nakai, H. and Saitō, S., 2016. *Rekishika no shiro aruki*. Tokyo: Koshi shoin.

Nakai, H. and Kayumi Rekishi Henshūbu, eds, 2018. *Sengoku no meijo 50*. Tokyo: Takarajimasha.

10 Festivals of war

Travelling the Shinsengumi in 2019

Philip Seaton

In 2019 I attended the Hino Shinsengumi Festival in western Tokyo on 12 May and the Goryōkaku Festival in Hakodate on 18–19 May. Both festivals commemorate Shinsengumi, a corps of samurai loyal to the Tokugawa shogunate that was active from 1863 until the final defeat of shogunate forces at the Battle of Hakodate in May 1869. The focus is particularly on Hijikata Toshizō, vice-commander of Shinsengumi, who died fighting to the end in Hakodate. The festivals in 2019 marked the 150th anniversary of his death and Shinsengumi's demise.

The festivals meet Frost and Laing's (2013: 1) categorization of a commemorative event, namely one 'typically planned with intentions of affirming and reinforcing memories that provide a sense of heritage and identity'. Consequently, locations and timings matter. Hino is the birthplace of various Shinsengumi members; Hakodate is the deathplace of Hijikata and the corps; and both festivals are timed to coincide roughly with the anniversary of the final defeat of shogunate loyalists. However, the festivals are also designed to attract tourists and are held on weekends to ensure maximum tourist/community attendance.

War-related tourism continues year-round in Hino and Hakodate, often fitting the classic 'host–guest' format. Travellers from afar visit Shinsengumi-related monuments, memorials, museums, and battlefields, whether as part of the commemorative pilgrimage, educational-style heritage tourism, or as contents tourists (Figure 1.3). However, in their performative aspects, the festivals collapse or even reverse the 'host–guest' distinction. The festivals involve 're-enactments' and other performances. Festival participants/performers often come from afar, while many spectators are local residents. At the Hino Shinsengumi Festival in 2019, around 400 people in period dress participated in the parades. They came from all over the country and even abroad to take part, while many of the 50,000 people lining the streets as spectators were locals (Hino City 2021). At the Goryōkaku Festival one of the main events

DOI: 10.4324/9781003239970-12

is the Hijikata Contest, in which competitors perform Hijikata's death in battle. The winner and runner-up of the contest on 18 May 2019 were both from Tokyo. As part of their prize, they joined the parade the following day. Two Tokyo-based Shinsengumi fans in Hakodate as contents tourists became performers in a tourism event heavily aimed at local residents.

Both the Hino and Hakodate festivals contain 'mock battles' staged in the city's streets with tourists watching from the pavement. The jocularity during scenes of death and killing is notable. In Hino, Shinsengumi members danced and taunted the Restoration forces before being shot at. Then, the banter, dancing, and chanting started again to roars of laughter from the crowds. It was street theatre more than re-enactment. A week later, during the Hijikata Contest in Hakodate, while the winners were those who passionately acted the final moments of Hijikata before he was shot, one local group gave a performance resembling slapstick or pantomime. In the mock battle during the parade the following day, spectators cheered when Hijikata cut down the commander of the Restoration army forces. These levels of playfulness indicate that the festivals have gone beyond sombre commemoration of the war. Indeed,

Figure 10.1 The Goryōkaku Festival parade, 19 May 2019. War commemoration meets contents tourism: in the float is Yamamoto Kōji (right), the actor who played Hijikata Toshizō in NHK's 2004 Taiga drama *Shinsengumi!*. Author's photo.

it is unthinkable for such re-enactments to exist at municipal events for Japan's more recent wars. As Frost and Laing (2013: 82) observe in the western context, 're-enactments of recent wars are noticeably absent … It may be that battles from the last 100 years are still too dark and embedded in personal memories to be commemorated in this form'.

The light-hearted nature of the festivals is possible because of 'chronological distance' (Figure 1.4). But the composition of Shinsengumi contents within popular culture and collective memories is also significant. The festivals are fundamentally celebrations of local heroes and demonstrate the pride the community feels through association with them. Hino brands itself as the *furusato* ('hometown') of Shinsengumi. It has the municipal Shinsengumi Furusato Historical Museum and three private museums run by the families of Shinsengumi members: the Hijikata Toshizō Museum, Inoue Genzaburō Museum, and Sato Hikogorō and Shinsengumi Museum. Hakodate, meanwhile, embraces Shinsengumi as part of a broader association with Meiji Restoration history via its role as a treaty port in the 1850s and 1860s.

The Goryōkaku Festival clearly sides with the losing shogunate loyalists, despite Hakodate city having no particular need to identify with the defeated. Formal commemorative events take place at Hekketsuhi (a monument to shogunate loyalists killed in the battle) and the monument at the Ippongi Gate, where Hijikata is believed to have been killed (Figure 0.1). There are no equivalent commemorations at Hakodate Gokoku [nation-protecting] Shrine, where there are graves of Restoration army soldiers and where their souls are enshrined as *eirei* (glorious dead) for their death in the service of the imperial cause. Gokoku shrines mirror the function of the controversial Yasukuni Shrine (Chapter 15) at the local level. Any involvement would inevitably embroil the festival in contested interpretations and commemorations of Japan's twentieth-century wars.

Imagining Hijikata

Hijikata embodies unswerving loyalty and self-sacrifice to his cause. He chose a samurai's death rather than surrender. Lee also suggests that 'Hijikata is popularly imagined and loved as a hero driven by self-determination' (Lee 2011: 183). This popular image has been made possible by two intertwined processes.

The first is the broader narrative transformation of shogunate loyalists from 'traitors' immediately after the Restoration to 'heroes' in the twenty-first century. This was a lengthy process with the festivals only emerging in the latter stages. In Hino, local residents were long discouraged from publicizing their connections to Shinsengumi. The corps were on the losing side in Japan's last civil war and became *zoku-gun*, 'rebels', who had opposed the restoration of imperial rule. When Shinsengumi's leader Kondō Isami was captured, he was executed as a criminal in May 1868. Antipathy towards the rebels was also evident after the Battle of Hakodate, when the bodies of 800 defeated 'rebels' were left in the open to rot. Only in 1875 was the Hekketsuhi monument erected in a secluded woodland part way up Mt Hakodate to quietly commemorate the shogunate loyalists. By contrast, their fallen adversaries were buried and enshrined at Hakodate Gokoku Shrine as loyal servants of the emperor. However, after 1945 'victor's history' assumed new meanings. Gokoku shrines became tainted by their Asia-Pacific War associations. In this postwar environment, the city has chosen to focus commemorations during the festival at sites to the 'rebels', and not to Restoration forces.

The second process is the 'romanticization' (Lee 2011) of Shinsengumi in pop culture, and the transformation of individual Shinsengumi members from historical figures to *characters* (Chapter 1). In life, Hijikata earned an infamous reputation as the 'demon vice-commander' of Shinsengumi for using torture, being a fearless killer, and ordering the *seppuku* (ritual suicide) of Shinsengumi members breaking the group's code. The image make-over of Shinsengumi started in 1928 with the publication of the novel *Shinsengumi shimatsuki* by Shimozawa Kan. It accelerated with Shiba Ryōtarō's serialized novel *Moeyo ken* (published in the magazine *Shūkan bunshun* 1962–1964), which had Hijikata as the main character. From the 2000s, Hijikata and Shinsengumi appeared in the manga/anime *Gintama* (manga 2003–) and game/anime *Hakuoki* (2008–) among many other pop culture works. Hijikata's transformation to pop idol was completed on screen when he was played by Okada Junichi of pop group V6 in the 2021 film *Baragaki: Unbroken Samurai* (based on *Moeyo ken*).

Much of this contemporary pop idol (*aidoru*) image derives from the iconic portrait of Hijikata sitting casually in black western clothing. The original photo was smuggled back to Hino by Sato Hikogorō after Hijikata's death and is stored in the Sato Hikogorō and Shinsengumi Museum. To prevent deterioration, it is on display only during the festival, giving Hijikata fans added incentive to visit Hino at that time. This photo exemplifies how an authentic artefact may inspire the transformation of a historical figure into a character, spawn a 'usable narrative world' (Figure 1.3), and ultimately generate a (war-related) contents tourism phenomenon.

Shinsengumi's story, therefore, has metamorphosed over time not only in terms of its political/commemorative meanings but also in its value as the basis for pop culture contents and as a tourism resource. The festivals emerged within this context, although it took a century or more after 1869 for this to happen. The Goryōkaku Festival began in 1970. The first Hino festival was in 1988. By the 2020s, Shinsengumi had become pop culture icons. Its members are idolized; people openly refer to themselves as Shinsengumi 'fans' and post videos of their 'pilgrimages' to Shinsengumi 'sacred sites' on YouTube; cosplayers can be seen at pop culture events; and Shinsengumi imagery adorns a wide range of products from T-shirts to beer cans. Shinsengumi-related pop culture epitomizes how war can transform over time from brutal events to entertainment, and contemporary Shinsengumi tourism epitomizes how war-related entertainment cross-fertilizes tourist sites and events.

COVID-19 postscript

However, the festivals during the COVID-19 pandemic indicate that while the touristy elements of the festivals could be cancelled, the heritage elements could not. Hino cancelled its festival in 2020 but produced an online video (Hino City 2021) in lieu of the 2021 festival. It focused on heritage elements via, for example, interviews with the relatives of Shinsengumi members who run museums in the city. Hakodate, meanwhile, cancelled the parades and restricted the 2020–2021 festivals to invitation-only commemorative events at four sites including Hekketsuhi and Ippongi Gate. As such, these festivals constitute examples not only of how two communities have developed war-related events as part of a localized (contents) tourism policy but also how these events are underpinned by local heritage. It was this local heritage that sustained the festivals during the period when the pandemic precluded in-person tourism.

References

Frost, W. and Laing, J., 2013. *Commemorative events: memory, identities, conflicts.* London: Routledge.

Hino City, 2021. *Dai-24-kai Hino Shinsengumi Matsuri.* YouTube. https://youtu.be /mo4jRlwgKAM.

Lee, R., 2011. Romanticising Shinsengumi in contemporary Japan. *New Voices,* 4, 168–187. http://dx.doi.org/10.21159/nv.04.08.

Part III
Imperial Japan

11 Hokkaido as imperial acquisition and the Ainu in popular culture and tourism

Ryo Koarai

Following the Meiji Restoration (1868), Japan was involved in many overseas wars under the 'Rich country strong army' policy. Japan's colonization of Hokkaido was an important part of colonial policy to protect Japan's northern border with the Russian empire. One work depicting imperial Japan's northern area is the manga *Golden Kamuy* (2014–present) by Noda Satoru, which is set in Hokkaido and Sakhalin just after the Russo-Japanese War. One of the main characters is Sugimoto Saichi, a veteran of the Imperial Japanese Army, and another is Asirpa, an Ainu girl. The two join forces to search for hidden Ainu gold. In this action-adventure tale, they fight over the gold with other Ainu, former members of the Imperial Japanese Army, former members of Shinsengumi, and Russians. An anime television series based on manga extended to three series. The work is popular among both young men and especially women.

The story is set across much of Hokkaido and Sakhalin, including Otaru, Sapporo, Asahikawa, Abashiri, and southern Sakhalin. On the official anime home page, audiences can use an interactive feature to see where the action takes place in each episode (TV Anime *Golden Kamuy* Official Site 2020). The story includes some clearly fantastical elements, for example, one character is an elderly Hijikata Toshizō (who actually died during the Battle of Hakodate in 1869 – see Introduction; Chapter 10). But, in other ways the story attempts to be highly accurate or authentic: for example, it introduces Ainu culture in great detail and explains how the Ainu were affected by the Meiji government's imperialism in Hokkaido. It also depicts the Imperial Japanese Army Seventh Division, which was based in Hokkaido at that time.

Hokkaido is a popular Japanese destination for both domestic and international tourists. But how have fans travelled the narrative world of *Golden Kamuy*? And how does this contents tourism relate to Hokkaido war history?

DOI: 10.4324/9781003239970-14

Golden Kamuy tourism and Ainu culture

Fan tourism relating to *Golden Kamuy* typically involves experiencing traditional Ainu culture, including history, clothing, food, and housing. Many Ainu characters, including Asirpa, Inkarmat, Kiroranke, and others, appear in *Golden Kamuy*. The Ainu villages (*kotan* in the Ainu language) in the story are fictional, so tourists cannot visit them in real life. But tourists can gain insights into these characters by visiting general sites introducing Ainu culture, such as Upopoy, the National Ainu Museum and Park in Shiraoi, Hokkaido.

Tourists can also eat traditional Ainu dishes. *Golden Kamuy* has lengthy scenes introducing Ainu cuisine. Some of the dishes featured in the story, such as *citatap* and *ohaw*, are served at Ainu restaurants in Hokkaido. Fans go to try them out. One key effect of *Golden Kamuy*, therefore, is that fans are visiting Ainu restaurants. Although there are Ainu restaurants in Tokyo and Osaka serving the dishes that appear in *Golden Kamuy*, fans give special importance to dining experiences in Hokkaido. The traditional Ainu dishes appearing in *Golden Kamuy* are 'food and drink as paratexts' (Williams 2020: 155) for fans and have a connection with Hokkaido. When fans eat the Ainu dishes appearing in *Golden Kamuy* in Hokkaido, they connect contents and food, food and destination, and destination and contents. By doing so, the fans achieve strong 'immersion' (Jenkins 2006: 286) in the narrative world story.

Furthermore, some Ainu restaurants have displays about Ainu culture featuring items such as clothing and household items. Fans who travel to Hokkaido on the trail of *Golden Kamuy* can experience Ainu culture via dining experiences. The reverse pattern also exists. The National Ainu Museum and Park, Upopoy, has a restaurant called Hinna Hinna Kitchen. Most dishes served there are made with ingredients commonly used in Ainu dishes, but the phrase 'hinna hinna' often appears in *Golden Kamuy* when characters express gratitude for the food they are eating (Hadakadenkyu 2018). While the museum does not appear in *Golden Kamuy*, nevertheless fans can feel a connection to the narrative world and learn about Ainu culture there. In actuality, young fans visit the town of Shiraoi where Upopoy is located, and *Golden Kamuy* has influenced visitation rates (Seaton 2017).

Golden Kamuy tourism and the Imperial Japanese Army Seventh Division

Most fans of *Golden Kamuy* also visit sites linked to the Imperial Japanese Army, especially the Seventh Division, which was based in Hokkaido.

Golden Kamuy has many fictional characters connected with the Seventh Division and they are associated with sites in Otaru, Sapporo, and Asahikawa. For example, at the Hokkaido University Botanic Garden (Figure 11.1) fans can visit the building which was the model for a taxidermist's home that Lieutenant Tsurumi visited in *Golden Kamuy*. The Historical Village of Hokkaido, an open-air museum in Sapporo, also contains various historical buildings that were models for buildings in *Golden Kamuy*, and some of them relate to soldiers and army deserters from the Seventh Division.

These buildings appearing in *Golden Kamuy* were inspired by extant buildings, but in actual history the Seventh Division did not use them. Furthermore, *Golden Kamuy*'s characters in the Seventh Division are completely fictional. However, many fans gain an interest in the real Seventh Division by reading and watching *Golden Kamuy*. When these fans become tourists they can visit sites related to the real Seventh Division. Many fans visit the Hokuchin Memorial Museum in Asahikawa, a museum operated by the Japan Ground Self-Defense Force whose exhibits focus heavily on the prewar Seventh Division. Despite making no appearance in *Golden Kamuy*, the museum is introduced in some fan

Figure 11.1 The model for a taxidermist's home in *Golden Kamuy*. Author's photo.

blogs and YouTube videos (for example, Yuruyuru Hokkaido 2020) as a pilgrimage site for *Golden Kamuy* fans. At the Hokuchin Memorial Museum, there is a board signed by Noda Satoru on display and *Golden Kamuy* comics are put out for visitors to read. In addition, the museum has also put on a special exhibition for fans' visits (Minna no Asahikawa 2019).

As these examples demonstrate, fans visit buildings which were models for places in the story with no link with the real Seventh Division, and also places which do not appear in *Golden Kamuy* but are connected to the actual Seventh Division. However, using Godwin's (2017) understanding of fan tourism as a fan practice that is motivated by a tourist's desire to be closer to or to make the connection with a narrative world, it can be said that visitation to such sites is a form of fan tourism. In addition, these practices exemplify typical characteristics of contents tourism, whereby fans 'attempt to experience a fictional narrative world in the real physical world' (Yamamura 2021: 56).

Conclusion

Fans visit Hokkaido to see sites connected to *Golden Kamuy*, and during this tourism fans also experience Ainu culture, which was affected by the Meiji government's imperialism and the history of the real Seventh Division. As with other forms of fan tourism, *Golden Kamuy* tourism is motivated by tourists' desire to be closer to or to make a connection with a narrative world. Such visits are only for fun and give the appearance of being completely free of the more serious side of war-related tourism and war history. However, *Golden Kamuy* fan tourism also has the potential to overlap with heritage tourism, war-related tourism, and so-called dark tourism connected to Japanese imperialism through fans' desire to know more about the background to *Golden Kamuy*. This includes how the Ainu were affected by Japan's colonization of Hokkaido in the late nineteenth and early twentieth century, and the role of the real Seventh Division in the 'pacification of the north' (*hokuchin*, which is the name of the museum). This potential of *Golden Kamuy* fan tourism does not derive from fans' desire to consume war and imperialism as entertainment but instead derives from fans' respect for the culture and history related to *Golden Kamuy*.

References

Godwin, V., 2017. Theme park as interface to the wizarding (story) world of Harry Potter. *Transformative Works and Cultures*, 25. https://doi.org/10.3983/twc.2017.01078.

Hadakadenkyu, 2018. *Hinna hinna suru? Ainu ryōri wo honba Hokkaido de tannō!* Meshitu. https://www.hotpepper.jp/mesitsu/entry/hadakadenkyu/18-00204.

Jenkins, H., 2006. *Convergence culture: where old and new media collide.* New York: NYU Press.

Minna no Asahikawa, 2019. 'Gōruden Kamui' ni tōjō no daishichi shidan 'nichiro tokushu' ni fan zokuzoku Asahikawa Hokuchin kinenkan de tokubetsu tenji. *Minna no Asahikawa*, 3 December. https://medoasa.com/n-15/.

Seaton, P., 2017. Poroto Kotan. *International Journal of Contents Tourism*, 8 July 2017. https://contents-tourism.press/postcards/poroto-kotan/.

TV Anime Golden *Kamuy* Official Site, 2020. *Story.* TV anime Golden Kamuy official site. https://kamuy-anime.com/story/36.html.

Williams, R., 2020. *Theme park fandom: spatial transmedia, materiality and participatory cultures.* Amsterdam: Amsterdam University Press.

Yamamura, T., 2021. Kontentsu tsūrizumu de yomitoku kakuchō genjituka suru shakai: kakuchō shitsuzukeru monogatari sekai to tsūrizumu jissen ni tsuite. *In*: Y. Yamada and R. Okamoto, eds. *Ima watashitachi wo tsunagu mono: kakuchō genjitsu jidai no kankō to media.* Tokyo: Kōbundō, 41–60.

Yuruyuru Hokkaido, 2020. *'Gōruden kamui seichi junrei', dai-shichi shidan no ashiato, Hokuchin kinenkan wo tazunete.* YouTube. https://youtu.be/hM_1oujCMMU.

12 The Russo-Japanese War and (contents) tourism

Philip Seaton

The Russo-Japanese War exemplifies the phases that war history goes through before becoming a 'usable narrative world' (Figure 1.3) for the entertainment and leisure industries. Defeating a European power propelled Japan to great power status. Consequently, the Russo-Japanese War generated many positive conditions for inducing tourism activity (Figure 1.4). However, defeat in 1945 deprived Japan of its 1905 spoils of victory, such as Karafuto (now southern Sakhalin island), domination over the Korean peninsula, and control of the Kuriles (the southern portion of which is now controlled by Russia but claimed by Japan as its Northern Territories). Defeat in 1945 also discredited the Japanese empire, generating contested memories rather than a heroic, unifying narrative about the empire's 'finest hour'. But with the war now over a century into the past, the Russo-Japanese War has largely 'become history' and war-related contents tourism can flourish, albeit still with the power to divide.

In the aftermath of Japan's victory, there were large-scale public celebrations and military reviews. Millions visited exhibitions of the spoils of war in Yūshūkan Museum at Yasukuni Shrine (Chapter 15) or displayed in front of the Imperial Palace (Dickinson 2005: 525–528). Public interest in Russo-Japanese War films and domestic events quickly dwindled (Chiba 2007: 358–363), but victory triggered the first overseas tours in newly acquired spheres of influence after 1906. Battlefield tours (particularly of Hill 203 outside Port Arthur) and visits by schoolchildren were at the forefront of early post-victory tourism (Soyama 2019: 47; McDonald 2019). By 1918 there was an imperial travel industry as 'the empire's major transportation institutions joined with the Japan Tourist Bureau (JTB) to begin services for domestic travelers' (McDonald 2017: 57). In the aftermath of the First World War, attitudes towards war became more sombre. But in the 1930s Japan stopped observing Armistice Day (Dickinson 2005: 543) and 'memory of the Russo-Japanese War was

DOI: 10.4324/9781003239970-15

purposely rekindled' ahead of the outbreak of the Second World War (Chiba 2007: 363). From the late 1920s, and particularly for the 25th and 30th anniversaries of victory, there were many exhibitions featuring the Russo-Japanese War. Exhibitions were a popular cultural activity of the era and could attract a million visitors or more (Shimazu 2009: 241–248). During 1940, when there were many events celebrating the empire's 2,600th anniversary, Port Arthur was a 'holy' destination and there were daily bus tours in which the war-related sites were the 'primary tourist attraction' (Ruoff 2010: 131). All these tourism patterns fit the mould of war-related tourism as a patriotic act – imaginaries of (subjective) war experiences (Figure 1.3) – although the extensive popular culture relating to the war at the time could also have been triggering something akin to contents tourism. However, it would not be until well after the Second World War that Russo-Japanese War tourism unambiguously assumed a contents tourism element.

During the early period of tourism to 1940, the sites visited were primarily overseas battlefields (such as Port Arthur) or domestic commemorative sites including Yasukuni Shrine/Yūshūkan Museum, Nogi Shrine (honouring Nogi Maresuke, consecrated in 1923), Tōgō Shrine (honouring Tōgō Heihachirō, consecrated in 1940), and the battleship *Mikasa* (Tōgō's flagship at the Battle of Tsushima Straits). *HIJMS Mikasa* was decommissioned under the terms of the 1922 Washington Naval Conference and became a memorial ship in 1926 in a dry dock in the naval city of Yokosuka (Mikasa Preservation Society n.d.: 20). However, from 1942 until the 1960s, war and defeat effectively shut down Russo-Japanese War tourism. Japanese could not travel overseas for leisure until 1964 (making battlefield tours impossible); Yūshūkan was closed from 1945 to 1986; and *HIJMS Mikasa* was stripped of its guns and masts during the occupation before restoration work allowed it to reopen in 1961 (ibid.). Only the shrines remained accessible to the general public during this period.

Works of popular culture depicting the war underpinned the post-1945 recovery of Russo-Japanese War tourism. The first Russo-Japanese War film of the postwar era was *The Emperor Meiji and the Great Russo-Japanese War* (1957), which was also notable as the first film to feature an emperor as the leading character. This film was nationalistic, due to both the director's own right-wing views and the need to avoid the risks of lèse-majesté and violent backlash by right-wingers (Chiba 2007: 371–372). This film set the patriotic tone of post-1945 films about the Russo-Japanese War, in contrast to the prewar era, in which films about the Russo-Japanese War ranged from 'left-leaning films' to 'period dramas' to prowar 'commemoration films' (Shimazu 2009: 249–251). This range of political ideologies would be replicated in postwar films about the Asia–Pacific War. But after 1945 the Russo–Japanese War, as Japan's last great victory of the imperial era, gained a particular place in the hearts of conservative and nationalist filmmakers.

The defining moment in Russo–Japanese War tourism came in 1968–1972 with the publication of Shiba Ryōtarō's serialized novel *Clouds Above the Hill* in the *Sankei shinbun* newspaper. Shiba's novel 'established the orthodoxy for the post-1945 reconstruction of the 1904–5 war in popular cultural memory' (Shimazu 2009: 273). Shiba's 'view of history' (known as the *Shiba shikan*) was not explicitly 'nationalist' in that his positive assessment of the Meiji period co-existed with criticism of Japan's actions during the Second World War. Nevertheless, he does present the Russo–Japanese War as Japan pursuing its legitimate national interests, regardless of the consequences for Korea (Seaton 2021: 51, 54). This uplifting interpretation created a 'usable narrative world' (Figure 1.3) at the intersection of subjective patriotic history, heritage tourism, and Shiba fandom.

Most significantly, Shiba created a new 'sacred site' for Russo–Japanese War tourism: Matsuyama in Ehime prefecture. This was the hometown

Figure 12.1 The Akiyama Brothers' Birthplace Museum, Matsuyama. Shiba Ryōtarō's novel turned the brothers from little-known military men into iconic figures within Japanese memories of the Russo-Japanese War. Author's photo.

of the three main protagonists: Akiyama Yoshifuru, Akiyama Saneyuki, and poet Masaoka Shiki. From the early 2000s, the city has had a *machi-zukuri* (community building) project centred on Shiba's novel that has yielded clear tourism benefits to the city (Seaton 2021: 56). The Clouds Above the Hill Museum and the Akiyama Brothers' Birthplace Museum were built, and other sites were designated as part of the *Clouds Above the Hill* tourism itinerary. These sites were all opened in time to benefit from a tourism boom generated by NHK's dramatization of Shiba's novel in 2009–2011. This touristification process has not been uncontested at the local level, with concerns voiced about the ideologies behind the novel and drama (Seaton 2021). From a contents tourism perspective, however, the drama boosted visitation to heritage sites and also added shooting locations to the Russo-Japanese War tourism itinerary, in particular a bridge evocative of the Meiji period in Uchiko town (30 kilometres south of Matsuyama) and the Etajima Naval Academy in Hiroshima prefecture. Japanese visitation to Lushun (Port Arthur) also boomed as a result of the drama (McDonald 2019: 77). What might be termed the 'second phase' of Japanese tourism to battlefield sites in China, therefore, is largely underpinned by popular culture.

Whereas these historically based representations of the war induce contents tourism, another notable characteristic of Russo-Japanese War tourism is that forms are diversifying as the war recedes into the past. The manga/anime *Golden Kamuy* (Chapter 11) has generated war-related tourism to sites such as the Hokuchin Memorial Museum in Asahikawa. The manga/anime's opening sequence is the assault on Hill 203 and fans visit the museum, which has exhibits about Hill 203 given its significance within Imperial Army Seventh Division history. Furthermore, the decks of *HIJMS Mikasa* have become popular with cosplayer fans of the online game and anime *Kantai Collection* (Chapter 20), even though the game/anime is war fantasy rather than in a Russo-Japanese War scenario (Sugawa-Shimada 2019). And whereas Russo-Japanese War contents tourism is now primarily related to works that are conservative/nationalist eulogies to a Japanese victory, more critical works can generate tourism, too. Yosano Akiko's poem *Kimi shinitamō koto nakare* (Brother, do not give your life), published to much controversy in 1904, has been canonized as a classic work of Japanese anti-war poetry (Rabson 1991). Fans of Yosano, and more generally Japanese poetry, make pilgrimages to the Yosano Akiko Museum in her hometown of Sakai and other sites related to arguably Japan's most celebrated female poet.

In short, despite a 'chronological distance' (Chapter 1) of over 100 years removed from the present, the Russo-Japanese War has not yet completed its shift to a tourism imaginary of war-related entertainment.

Instead, the shifting patterns of tourism since 1905 demonstrate neatly how it is not only the nature of the war being depicted in works of entertainment that matters. It is also the social, cultural, and political milieu of the postwar, pre-next-war, and post-next-war that shape the tourism flows generated by war.

References

Chiba, I., 2007. Shifting contours of memory and history, 1904–1980. *In*: D. Wolff et al., eds. *The Russo-Japanese war in global perspective: World War Zero – volume II.* Leiden: Brill, 355–378.

Dickinson, F.R., 2005. Commemorating the war in post-Versailles Japan. *In*: J.W. Steinberg et al., eds. *The Russo-Japanese war in global perspective: World War Zero.* Leiden: Brill, 523–543.

McDonald, K., 2017. *Placing empire: travel and the social imagination in imperial Japan.* Berkeley: University of California Press.

McDonald, K., 2019. War, firsthand, at a distance: battlefield tourism and conflicts of memory in the multiethnic Japanese empire. *Japan Review*, 33, 57–85.

Mikasa Preservation Society, n.d. *Memorial ship Mikasa.* Yokosuka: Mikasa Preservation Society.

Rabson, S., 1991. Yosano Akiko on war: to give one's life or not – a question of which war. *Journal of the Association of Teachers of Japanese*, 25 (1), 45–74.

Ruoff, K.J., 2010. *Imperial Japan at its zenith: the wartime celebration of the empire's 2,600th anniversary.* Ithaca: Cornell University Press.

Seaton, P., 2021. The 'Shiba view of history' and Japan-Korea relations: reading, watching and travelling *Clouds Above the Hill. In*: R. Sakamoto and S. Epstein, eds. *Popular culture and the transformation of Japan-Korea relations.* London: Routledge, 48–60.

Shimazu, N., 2009. *Japanese society at war: death, memory and the Russo-Japanese war.* Cambridge: University of Cambridge Press.

Soyama, T., 2019. School excursions and militarism: continuities in tourist *shūgaku ryokō* from the Meiji period to the postwar. *Japan Review*, 33, 29–56.

Sugawa-Shimada, A., 2019. Playing with militarism in/with *Arpeggio* and *Kantai Collection*: effects of *shōjo* images in war-related contents tourism in Japan. *Journal of War & Culture Studies*, 12 (1), 53–66.

13 Tourism relating to the new culture introduced by First World War German POWs

Kyungjae Jang

During the First World War, Japan fought on the side of its ally Great Britain against Germany. The transportation to Japan of German prisoners captured in the Shandong peninsula of China enabled the expansion of German culture in Japan. Memories of those times have been kept alive through works of popular culture, and related places are consumed as tourism sites.

About 4,700 German and Austrian soldiers were taken as prisoners in the Japanese–German War, which ended with Germany's surrender. The prisoners were transferred to 12 camps around the country, mainly in western Japan (Seto 2013; Utsumi 2005). Japan's treatment of these prisoners was different from that meted out to prisoners of wars fought by Japan before the First World War, specifically the Sino-Japanese War of 1894–1895 and the Russo-Japanese War of 1904–1905. Owing to the short duration of the war, there was low hostility towards the German prisoners. Furthermore, Germany was thought of as a civilized Western European country, and German POWs were welcomed in Japan (Utsumi 2005: 93). At the ports where the prisoners entered the country, people waved Japanese and German flags and welcomed them with flowers. Some regions actively hosted prisoners with the aim of utilizing the Germans' technological skills to boost the regional economy (ibid. 98). The Japanese acceptance of German prisoners of war was the first modern experience of such kind, and this acceptance became the basis of future cultural exchange between Japan and Germany.

The German prisoners in most camps received warm treatment. In many camps, prisoners formed communities and interacted with local residents, teaching them various skills, sharing their technical knowledge, and teaching about vegetable cultivation and cooking methods (Utsumi 2005). They were allowed to venture out of the camp boundaries twice a week, and some even went on excursions. Seto (2013) describes life in

DOI: 10.4324/9781003239970-16

the Ninoshima Prison Camp in Hiroshima prefecture, where the prisoners published newspapers, held lectures, and organized craft exhibitions, theatre, artistic and sports activities, and excursions. Barring the compulsory labour, it was difficult to think of these Germans as prisoners of war.

Meanwhile, the Bando Prison Camp, which was established in Naruto city in 1917 by merging the Tokuyama, Marugame, and Matsuyama camps, had a bowling alley, a printing shop, and even a beer hall. It also had its own currency that could only be used in the camp. But, it was the orchestra that made the Bando Prison Camp famous. The first full-length performance in Japan of Beethoven's Symphony No. 9 was given in the camp (Utsumi 2005: 100–101). The 2006 film *Baruto no gakuen* (Ode to Joy) was made based on this story. Sets were constructed over a six-month period in Bando, where the camp was located. After filming had finished, it was opened to the public on 21 March 2006 under the name Bando Location Village. By 2009, when it closed, it had been visited by about 260,000 tourists. The tour guides in the location village introduced the history of the camp and the story behind the filming (Nakatani 2007: 45–46). It is a noteworthy example of the combination of memories of war, entertainment, and tourism.

On 26 December 1919, a year after the conclusion of the war, Japan announced the repatriation of its German prisoners of war. Although many prisoners returned to their home country or Qingdao, China, 171 chose to remain in Japan. Some prisoners used their skills and experience gained in captivity to establish food businesses. They made items that were not popular in Japan at the time, including ham, sausages, and bread. Some of these establishments continue to operate in Japan to this day.

The dramatic stories of these people who settled in Japan after their captivity are still talked about. Examples of such entrepreneurs include August Lohmeyer (1892–1962), who introduced *rōsuhamu* (sirloin ham), and Karl Juchheim (1886–1945), who turned Baumkuchen into a popular cake in Japan.

Lohmeyer worked in the meat processing industry before the war. He enlisted in the Navy in 1914 and went to China, where he was taken prisoner (Schmidt Muraki 2009). While in captivity, he served as a cook in the Kumamoto and Kurume prison camps. After the war, Lohmeyer remained in Japan and invented *rōsuhamu*, a Japanese-style ham made from sirloin. The livestock industry in Japan was not developed, and making ham from pork leg was technically difficult and costly. Instead, Lohmeyer made rolls of meat from the back and loins, which were not used at the time. They were processed into ham and called *rōsuhamu*. His company continued to operate after the war and was taken over by his son. It still exists today having survived for over a century.

Baumkuchen is another item introduced by German prisoners to Japan. Literally meaning 'wooden cake' or 'tree cake', Baumkuchen is a traditional cake from Eastern Germany. It is not commonly found in other countries, yet has become popular in patisseries across Japan. Karl Juchheim, a German working in a confectionery store in Qingdao, did not participate in the fighting but was tried for the possession of a military register. During his time as a prisoner, in 1919 he baked and sold Baumkuchen at the Ninoshima German Crafts Fair held at the Hiroshima Prefectural Commercial Exhibition Hall (Seto 2013: 12). It was the first time Baumkuchen was made in Japan. After the First World War, he settled in Kobe to make Baumkuchen under the label Juchheim, which his wife took over after his death on 14 August 1945 (Etajima 1973: 240). Juchheim is still Japan's leading Baumkuchen producer.

Incidentally, the Hiroshima Prefectural Commercial Exhibition Hall, where Juchheim first baked Baumkuchen, was at the hypocentre of the atomic bomb explosion on 6 August 1945. It is known now as the Atomic Bomb Dome and is designated as a UNESCO World Heritage Site. A place where a humanely treated prisoner introduced a new food into Japan after the First World War became a symbol of the tragedy and cruelty of war after the Second World War.

But perhaps the most dramatic case is that of Heinrich Freundlieb (1884–1955), whose story was fictionalized in a TV drama based on the experiences of prisoners of war. Freundlieb, who established a bakery in Qingdao in 1912 after retiring from the Navy, was conscripted again in 1914. He participated in the fighting but was taken prisoner and sent to a camp in Nagoya. After the war, he married a Japanese woman and worked as the first baker at the Shikishima Bakery Company founded in Nagoya in 1920. He later settled in Kobe in 1924 to run his own bakery and restaurant.

In 1977, NHK's morning drama series *Kazamidori* (The Weather Vane) was based on his life. The exotic Western-style architecture of Kobe combined with an unusual story of an international marriage in the First World War period caused interest in the drama and a tourism boom in Kitano ward in Kobe, the main location of the series (Jang 2019). The weather vane on the roof of Freundlieb's bakery became a symbol of Kobe and the broadcast date of the first episode, 3 October, was designated as Kobe Tourism Day. The house where Freundlieb lived was inherited by

Figure 13.1 Former Freundlieb house, Kobe. Author's photo.

his son, who later operated the bakery. The second floor was used as a memorial room until the 1995 Great Hanshin Earthquake. Owing to the damage caused by the earthquake, the building was donated to the city, and now, following renovations, is used as a café.

Of course, the examples introduced in this chapter should not make us overlook the fact that painful memories of war have been beautifully repackaged. There were also numerous instances of prisoners of war who were treated severely. Nevertheless, the story of German prisoners in the First World War is an example of how war can generate peaceful cultural exchange that underpins cultural, culinary, and contents tourism even a century after the war.

References

Etajima, I., 1973. *Kāru Yūhaimu monogatari: kashi wa kamisama.* Tokyo: Shinsensha.
Jang, K., 2019. Tourism and local identity generated by NHK's morning drama: the intersection of memory and imagination in Kobe. *East Asian Journal of Popular Culture*, 5 (2), 159–176.

Nakatani, T., 2007. Firumu tsūrizumu ni kansuru ichikōsatsu: 'kankō-chi imēji' no kōchiku to kankō keiken o megutte. *Nara Prefectural University Kenkyū kihō*, 18 (1 and 2), 41–56.

Schmidt Muraki, M., 2009. *Rōsuhamu no tanjō: Augusuto Rōmaiyā monogatari*. Tokyo: Ronsosha.

Seto, T., 2013. Daiichiji taisen-ji no Ninoshima furyo shūyōjo. *Bulletin of Hiroshima City Archives*, 26, 9–14.

Utsumi, A., 2005. *Nihongun no horyo seisaku*. Tokyo: Aoki Shoten.

14 Theatre (contents) tourism and war as a backdrop to romance

Akiko Sugawa-Shimada

Wars and natural disasters are often used as story backdrops because of their dramatic moments and the opportunities for *deus ex machina* plot twists, especially in romance stories. Often in contents tourism, the more that readers/audiences are moved by dramatic stories, the more they are motivated to visit related locations. This chapter examines two instances of war as a backdrop for romance stories that have triggered theatre (contents) tourism. Theatre going can often be considered to be tourism, especially when a theatre district forms a key part of a destination's appeal (such as Broadway or London's West End), or when fans travel long distances and stay overnight to attend performances. The two case studies in this chapter are of stage productions that form part of transmedia franchises, making theatre tourism contents tourism. Theatre tourism among young people in Japan is often induced by stage adaptations of narrative worlds originating in manga, anime, and videogames (Sugawa-Shimada 2020: 128).

The first example is *Samurai X* (*Rurouni Kenshin: Meiji swordsman romantic story*). *Samurai X* was a manga for boys by Watsuki Nobuhiro serialized from 1994 to1999 in *Weekly Shōnen Jump*, although it was also quite popular among women (Watsuki 1994). The story takes place in Tokyo in 1878. Himura Kenshin, a wanderer (*rurouni*), meets a cute girl, Kamiya Kaoru. She has taken over Kamiya kendo school in Tokyo after her parents' death. Kenshin's old nickname is Assassin Battōsai (lit. 'master of drawing a sword'). He killed a number of samurais loyal to the Tokugawa shogunate during the Bakumatsu period (1853–1868) and Boshin War (1868–1869), but he has taken an oath not to kill anybody since the Meiji Restoration.

Some actual events and historical figures are used in the story. For instance, Saitō Hajime, an actual ex-Shinsengumi member, is a lifelong rival of Kenshin; and a fictional character, Sagara Sanosuke, who

DOI: 10.4324/9781003239970-17

becomes Kenshin's friend, is an ex-Sekihō Army member.[1] Sagara Sōzō, the leader of the Sekihō Army, who in actual history was executed by the Meiji government, is Sanosuke's mentor. By using the battles of the Bakumatsu period and the Boshin War as backdrops, the story depicts how Kenshin atones for his past deeds and is saved psychologically by Kaoru's dedication to him and through his romance with her.

Samurai X was adapted into a TV anime (1996–1998), anime film (1997), original anime videos (1999–2012), live-action films (2012–2021), and musicals (2016; 2018). The live-action films featured a popular young actor, Satō Takeru, as Kenshin. This prompted both domestic and international fans to do film-location tourism in Shiga, Kyoto, Nara, Shizuoka, and Tochigi prefectures. The official website of the final two films, *Rurouni Kenshin The Final/The Beginning*, has a film-location map which covers over 43 location sites in 12 prefectures (Warner Brothers 2021).

Samurai X also induced theatre tourism. The 2016 musical, *Roman katsugeki Rurouni Kenshin*, was directed by Koike Shuichiro of the Takarazuka Revue[2] and staged at the Takarazuka theatres in Hyogo prefecture and Tokyo. Koike's 2018 version was produced by Shochiku and Umeda Art Theatre, and was performed at Shinbashi Enbujo Theatre in Tokyo and Osaka Shochikuza Theatre. Both musicals cast the same actress, Sagiri Seina, as Kenshin, although other roles were played by different actors. Whereas fans of Takarazuka tend to be female, the audience for Shochiku's 2018 version was demographically varied. Some were fans of the manga and anime *Samurai X*, some were Sagiri Seina fans, and some were fans of Kamishiraishi Moka, an up-and-coming actress who played the role of Kaoru.

Watching this play at the theatre in 2018, it was notable how the production focused on how human drama and romance were influenced by battles in the Bakumatsu period and Boshin War, rather than focusing on action scenes. For instance, Kenshin rescues Kaoru after she is kidnapped by Kanō Sōzaburō, a fictional ex-Shinsengumi member who does not appear in the original manga. Kaoru stops a furious Kenshin from trying to kill Kanō, which ultimately leads to Kenshin feeling even more affection towards her. Here conflict and the introduction of a new character for the stage adaptation were used primarily to intensify the love story. While fans have many reasons to visit theatres, in this case, theatre (contents) tourism appears to be about consuming a romantic story rather than a war-related story. Even so, the wartime backdrop clearly gives tourism linked to the productions an element of war-related contents tourism.

Another example is *Here Comes Miss Modern* (*Haikara-san ga tōru*), Yamato Waki's comics for girls (1975–1977). The term *haikara-san* (a person wearing a high collar) was coined in late nineteenth-century Japan to refer to a liberal-minded person strongly affected by Western culture. It was often used sarcastically by those who favoured Japanese traditional culture. *Here Comes Miss Modern* was adapted into a TV anime (1978–1979), TV dramas (1985; 2002), a live-action film (1987), theatrical plays (1978; 1980; 1991; 1995), anime films (2017; 2018), and a musical by the Takarazuka Revue (2017; rerun in 2020).

The Taisho period (1912–1926) is associated with the liberal movement, Taisho democracy, and the romanticism art movement (*Taishō roman*). This resonated with the women's liberation movement in the 1970s when the manga *Here Comes Miss Modern* was serialized in the girls' manga magazine *Weekly Shōjo Friend*. Many liberal young female readers admired Benio, who is a strong, thoughtful, and independent girl. She works as a journalist and marries an *ikemen* (hunk) with half-Western roots. However, the Taisho period is also when Imperial Japan expanded its military presence into Russia (Siberia) and China after victory in the 1904–1905 Russo-Japanese War. The plot of *Here Comes Miss Modern* deftly utilizes these sociocultural and political upheavals to dramatize the separation and miraculous reunion of Benio and Shinobu.

The anime films were released in two parts: the first was released in 2017 and covered the story from Benio's encounter with Shinobu to her arrival in Manchuria; the second part was released the following year and covered from Benio's time in Manchuria to the happy ending. The films tied up with Butai Meguri ('visiting the stage'), a Sony smartphone app utilizing GPS to indicate the locations of *Here Comes Miss Modern*. This app prompts fans to visit 'sacred sites' in Tokyo, Yokohama, and Fukuoka. Interestingly, it also pins several 'tie-up' places that collaborated with the movies on the map, such as Japan Taisho Village (JTV, an attraction in Gifu prefecture that has preserved buildings built in the Taisho period, Figure 14.1) and Taisho Roman Dream Street in Kawagoe city, Saitama prefecture. Although they have nothing to do with the story, they were chosen as places where fans/audiences can feel the atmosphere of the Taisho period.

JTV ran a collaborative campaign called 'Taisho Roman de kyun' (literally 'heart-strings tugged by Taisho Romanticism') with the film *Here Comes Miss Modern* from September to December in 2017. Visitors could wander around JTV in a rental kimono with blue and white arrow-feather patterns and *hakama* trousers like those worn by Benio (Yoshioka 2017). Although Shinobu wore a Japanese Imperial Army uniform

Figure 14.1 Taisho Romankan hall, Japan Taisho Village. © PhotoAC/HiC

in the campaign poster and cardboard cutouts displayed around JTV, Shinobu's uniform was not for rent. Neither Japan's role in the Siberian Intervention nor the Russo-Japanese War were described in the *Here Comes Miss Modern* exhibition in the JTV museum, which avoided any connections to Japan's wars in the story. Instead, JTV targeted women who identify with Benio and enjoy the atmosphere of Taisho Roman that JTV provides.

The 1923 Great Kanto Earthquake also had a pivotal role in the plot. Approximately 69,000 people died or were missing in Tokyo alone (Disaster Management 2006: 114). The number of Korean and Chinese residents killed by Japanese mobs in the earthquake's aftermath is reported to be in the thousands. However, the musical avoids such negative incidents. The earthquake is rather divine intervention, leading Shinobu to find Benio in a collapsed church which is on fire due to the earthquake. The earthquake, like the history of the Siberian Intervention, is used as a device to enhance dramatic moments in the romance between Shinobu and Benio.

While the plots, wars, periods, and themes of the works vary, both narrative worlds have in common the plot device of wars and battles being used as backdrops to emphasize the protagonists' hardships.

Furthermore, the extreme circumstances of war help the lovers to come together in the end. Both *Samurai X* and *Here Comes Miss Modern* are successful transmedia franchises that have included theatrical adaptations, and have therefore induced theatre contents tourism. The plays are somewhat different, however, from Kuramoto Sō's *Kikoku* (Chapter 15), which focuses directly on war themes (rather than having war as a backdrop). The two case studies in this chapter are also distinguishable on a narrative level from the yōkai stories in Chapter 21. In Mizuki Shigeru's manga, war is always in the background, but in a metaphorical and unspoken way rather than as an explicit backdrop to the plot. The various examples indicate how wars exist on a sliding scale from 'centre stage', to 'backdrop', to 'behind the scenes' in the narrative worlds of war-related popular culture, and therefore war-related tourism, too.

Notes

1 Sekihō Army was a group of political extremists formed during Boshin War with the support of Saigō Takamori and Iwakura Tomomi of the new Meiji government.

2 The Takarazuka Revue is a women-only theatrical troupe founded in 1914. It has its own theatres in Takarazuka city, Hyogo, and Tokyo.

References

Disaster Management, 2006. *Saigai kyōkun no keishō ni kansuru senmon chōsakai hōkokusho: 1923 Kantō daishinsai*. Cabinet Office, Government of Japan. http://www.bousai.go.jp/kyoiku/kyokun/kyoukunnokeishou/rep/1923_kanto_daishinsai/pdf/1923--kantoDAISHINSAI-1_07_chap4.pdf.

Sugawa-Shimada, A, 2020. The 2.5-dimensional theatre as a communication site: non-site-specific theatre tourism. *In*: T. Yamamura and P. Seaton, eds. *Contents tourism and pop culture fandom: transnational tourist experiences*. Bristol: Channel View Publications, 128–143.

Warner Brothers, 2021. *Rokechi map*. Warner Brothers. https://wwws.warnerbros.co.jp/rurouni-kenshin2020/orocomm/map.html.

Watsuki, N., 1994. *Rurouni Kenshin: Meiji kenkaku roman tan*. Vol. 2. Tokyo: Shueisha.

Yoshioka, M., 2017. Gifu: anime eiga Haikara-san ga tōru to renkei Nihon Taisho mura. *Chunichi Shinbun*. 17 September. https://tabi.chunichi.co.jp/odekake/170927odekake_3.html.

Part IV

The Asia-Pacific War

15 Yasukuni Shrine's Yūshūkan museum as a site of contents tourism

Philip Seaton and Takayoshi Yamamura

In February 2021, a social media storm erupted when voice actress Kayano Ai, star of numerous anime including the 2020 hit *Demon Slayer*, said she visited Yasukuni Shrine on YouTube. Following heavy criticism, particularly from Chinese fans, Kayano withdrew the video and posted an apology for her 'lack of knowledge' (*chishiki busoku*) on her website (Kayano 2021). This is not the first such controversy. From 25 March to 6 April 2017, the Chiyoda Sakura Festival held a stamp rally in collaboration with the popular game *Tōken Ranbu-ONLINE* (Chapter 8). Yasukuni Shrine was one of the places to collect a stamp, eliciting strong criticism from some fans on social media, especially in China. Even so, Yasukuni Shrine is considered a sacred place by many Japanese fans of *Tōken Ranbu* because its museum, Yūshūkan, displays Japanese swords.

Yasukuni Shrine apotheosizes the souls of 2.46 million people who died during wars from the Meiji Restoration to the Pacific War and is a flashpoint in Sino-Japanese and Korean-Japanese relations. The Kayano and *Tōken Ranbu* furores indicate the tensions that can flare when the 'history issue' clashes with the Cool Japan policy (Chapter 1). It is conceivable, however, that some Kayano fans of a nationalistic persuasion became bigger fans as a result of the controversy and took the opportunity to (re)visit Yasukuni. Conversely, some Chinese fans of either Kayano or *Tōken Ranbu* might visit Yasukuni Shrine in the future to understand better this controversial war-related site for themselves. In both scenarios, visitation to Yasukuni Shrine contains an element of contents tourism.

We make an important distinction here between contents tourism and media tourism. Media tourism, in our formulation, includes tourism induced by non-fiction media such as television news, travel shows, documentaries (including the 2007 documentary film *Yasukuni* by Chinese director Li Ying), and social media. Contents tourism, by contrast, is

DOI: 10.4324/9781003239970-19

induced by creative works of entertainment that have no specific aim of inducing tourism. Such works may be historically accurate but appeal to fans because they are entertaining rather than because they are accurate. Contents tourism at Yasukuni Shrine, therefore, occurs when people visit Yasukuni Shrine as a setting for a scene in a movie, or as a shooting location, or as a site that is somehow significant within a 'narrative world' created by a (semi-) fictionalized work of entertainment.

Despite its contemporary image as a controversial war-related site, Yasukuni Shrine actually has a history as a place of entertainment. It was founded in 1869 as Tokyo Shōkonsha to commemorate those who fell in the cause of the Meiji Restoration. The Shrine quickly became a *meisho* – 'famous place' or tourist attraction (Takenaka 2015: 57-73). Yūshūkan, the Shrine's military museum, opened in 1882 in a building resembling a medieval Italian castle. The grounds hosted festivals, circuses, horse racing, and sumo competitions. After Japan's major victories in the First Sino-Japanese War and Russo-Japanese War, the Shrine put on victory spectaculars, although the heavy casualties during these wars accentuated the Shrine's original function of honouring the war dead. Swollen with new exhibits captured during Japan's victorious wars, Yūshūkan attracted over 10 million visitors per year in 1904–1906 (Takenaka 2015: 67).

Yasukuni's popularity meant it featured in the popular culture of the day. 'Yasukuni's circuses are well known for the literature they inspired, such as Kawabata Yasunari's "Shōkonsai ikkei" (A View of the *Shōkon* Ritual) and Yasuoka Shōtarō's "Sākasu no uma" (The Circus Horse)' and the Shrine is an important location in Futabatei Shimei's 1906 novel *Sono omokage* (The Adopted Husband) (Takenaka 2015: 62, 64). Such novels may continue to inspire visitation to Yasukuni today, as do modern works that use Yasukuni as a setting. One such work is Kuramoto Sō's 2009 play *Kikoku* (Returning home), which was made into the TBS war end special drama broadcast on 14 August 2010. A group of Japanese soldiers who died in a *gyokusai* (banzai charge) return as *eirei* (lit. 'glorious spirits', i.e. the war dead enshrined at Yasukuni) to see what has become of the places they knew as young men, and to reflect on whether present-day Japan is really what they thought they were dying to protect. One place the soldiers visit is Yasukuni Shrine, which appears as both the historical site to which Japan's soldiers were told their souls would return if they died and as a shooting location. Unsurprisingly, given that Yasukuni Shrine allowed filming on its grounds, the drama is conservative in tone. In one scene shot at the Shrine, two soldiers express frustration that today's political leaders cannot pay their respects at the Shrine without causing controversy.

After the war, Yasukuni lost its image as a tourist site, except as a spot for cherry blossom viewing. Yūshūkan was closed and only reopened in

1986. Following refurbishment in 2002, the entrance hall contains four main exhibits: two artillery pieces, a Zero fighter, and a locomotive. The locomotive was one of the first to travel the Thai–Burma Railroad, which some visitors might connect to the 1957 film *The Bridge on the River Kwai* or the 2013 film *The Railway Man*, although any contents tourism is likely to be incidental or serendipitous: i.e. visitors make the connection on seeing the engine rather than specifically going to Yūshūkan to see it. The Zero fighter, however, is of interest to fans of aviation movies ranging from the numerous naval action adventure films made since the 1950s to Studio Ghibli's 2013 anime *The Wind Rises*. Similar comments can be made about the other exhibits of military hardware in the Great Exhibition Hall, and the samurai swords on display in Exhibition Rooms 1 and 2.

The greatest opportunity for war-related contents tourism, however, is when one of the enshrined war dead has featured as a character in works of entertainment. The following heroes/characters/*eirei* are profiled in *Record in Pictures of Yasukuni Jinja Yūshūkan*, the official museum English guidebook (Yasukuni Shrine 2009):

- Sakamoto Ryōma, Yoshida Shōin, and other imperial loyalists of the Meiji Restoration feature extensively in television dramas, historical novels, and other works, and are widely utilized as tourism resources in their home prefectures.
- The two major heroes of the Russo-Japanese War, Nogi Maresuke and Tōgō Heihachirō, are not enshrined at Yasukuni because they did not die in battle. But, a scene of Nogi receiving notification of the death of his two sons is a staple of Russo-Japanese War films and Nogi's sons are profiled in Yūshūkan. There is also a memorial to Hirose Takeo, a major character in *Clouds Above the Hill* (Chapter 12).
- The 'Three human bombs' of the 1932 Shanghai incident, who blew themselves up to make a hole in a barbed wire obstacle, were eulogized in plays, films, and patriotic songs in the 1930s. This generated contents tourism at Yasukuni Shrine decades before the term was coined.
- Admiral Yamamoto Isoroku, Commander-in-Chief of the Combined Fleet and mastermind behind Pearl Harbor and Midway, died in April 1943. He has featured in many navy films and screen biopics.
- The stories and final letters of members of the kamikaze, kaiten, and other special attack units are displayed prominently in Yūshūkan. Kamikaze films have also generated considerable contents tourism at sites in southern Kyushu (Chapter 18).

- Kuribayashi Tadamichi was in command of the garrison on Iwo Jima. He was played by Watanabe Ken in the 2006 film *Letters from Iwo Jima*.
- The Himeyuri Corps of student nurses has featured in numerous films and dramas about the Battle of Okinawa. The girls who died are enshrined at Yasukuni and commemorated in the museum exhibits.
- The nine telephone operators of Maoka Post Office on Karafuto (now Sakhalin) who committed suicide in the face of the Soviet advance on 20 August 1945 have featured in various films and dramas, such as the 1974 film *Karafuto 1945-nen natsu, Hyōsetsu no mon* (Karafuto Summer of 1945: Gate of Ice and Snow).
- What Yasukuni Shrine calls the 'Showa era martyrs' are better known in English as the class-A war criminals. Tōjō Hideki and others executed after their conviction at the Tokyo Trials have featured in various works including the nationalistic 1998 film *Pride: unmei no toki* and a four-part NHK television drama in 2016. And while he is not an enshrined *eirei*, Indian judge Radhabinod Pal, who gave a famous dissenting judgement at the Tokyo Trials and was a major character in *Pride*, is honoured with a monument close to the entrance of Yūshūkan.

Figure 15.1 The temporary exhibition in Yūshūkan about composer Koseki Yūji. Photo: Yamamura Takayoshi.

- There is an exhibition of bridal dolls given to the museum by bereaved families of soldiers who died before getting married. These dolls represent a common trope of Japanese war stories: the sweetheart left behind on the home front by the soldier who goes off to war. One such character appeared in *Kikoku* described above. When the spirit of the soldier returns to visit the sweetheart he promised to marry, he finds her as an old woman who never loved another man. The dolls, and such characters in war stories, epitomize a conservative trope of a woman's pure love for a soldier who sacrificed all for family and nation.

Finally, in addition to its permanent exhibits, Yūshūkan has temporary exhibitions. From September to December 2020, there was an exhibition about composer Koseki Yūji, who composed the 1964 Olympic March, but also numerous patriotic songs before and during the Second World War. Koseki was the model for the main character in NHK's morning drama *Yell*, which aired from 30 March to 27 November 2020. This exhibition was created to attract contents tourists interested in the morning drama.

Yūshūkan, therefore, is full of 'contents', namely the stories of individuals who have featured as characters in works of popular culture entertainment. This makes Yasukuni Shrine and Yūshūkan into *seichi* or 'sacred sites' in two senses: the first is nationalistic, namely Yasukuni as a place where national martyrs are enshrined; the second relates to contents tourism, namely a place where fans of war-related entertainment can further their interest in via tourism. For Japanese with nationalistic inclinations, these ideas of *seichi* are compatible and mutually reinforcing. However, as the Kayano Ai and *Tōken Ranbu* controversies at the start of this chapter indicated, political ideologies and fandom can clash, such as when a Chinese fan's favourite Japanese voice actress visits the reviled Yasukuni Shrine. Nowhere more than the sacred site Yasukuni Shrine better reveals the tensions inherent between Japanese popular culture representations of war, the Cool Japan strategy, and contents tourism.

References

Kayano, A., 2021. *'Kayano Ai no musunde hiraite' dai-152-kai ni tsukimashite.* Kayano Ai, news post, 17 February 2021. https://kayanoai-10th-anniversary.com/news/.

Takenaka, A., 2015. *Yasukuni Shrine: history, memory, and Japan's unending postwar.* Honolulu: Hawai'i University Press.

Yasukuni Shrine, 2009. *Record in pictures of Yasukuni Jinja Yūshūkan.* Tokyo: Yasukuni Shrine.

16 The sense of belonging created by *In This Corner of the World*

Luli van der Does

The commercial and artistic success of the 2016 animation film *Kono sekai no katasumi ni* (*In This Corner of the World*) directed by Katabuchi Sunao was an unexpected boon for tourism in the cities of Kure and Hiroshima, where the film's story was set. Tourists and fans of the film make sacred site pilgrimages to locations in the story. Furthermore, according to fans and tourists, the film gives you an *ibasho*, or a place where you belong. This chapter discusses the sense of *ibasho* as a powerful form of motivation in contents tourism.

In the tourist imagination, Kure is a navy port city, and Hiroshima is the atomic-bombed peace city. Despite being only about 40 minutes apart by train, tourists rarely visit both cities, partly because their contrasting images of 'military' and 'peace' differentiate the motivations of tourists. This, however, gives a false impression of separation. Both communities were built around the military (Hiroshima was an important army base), and they were closely linked politically, socio-economically, and by population movements between them. In *In This Corner of the World*, Suzu, the daughter of a seaweed farmer in Hiroshima, marries Shūsaku, a clerical officer at the Kure Naval Base. The film depicts Suzu's life for 12 years from her childhood in Hiroshima to her married life in wartime Kure, and ends with her adopting a girl in the ruins of Hiroshima. Thus, Suzu's life links these two cities.

In Kure, fans of Suzu (known also as KonoSeka Walkers) follow in her trail from the bayside, past the Sawahara family's house with its famous triple warehouses (known as Mitsukura), up to her home high on the slopes of Haigamine Hill. Another popular route leads to the downtown areas and Asahi-machi, a former red-light district that Suzu mistakenly wanders into and where she first meets Lin, a courtesan and former lover of Shūsaku. Then the trail continues to the Nikō park, where Suzu happens on Lin again viewing cherry blossoms. Before Lin disappears in an air raid, she leaves Suzu a message of encouragement: 'You won't lose

DOI: 10.4324/9781003239970-20

your place in this world [*ibasho*] that easily'. These words echo at crucial moments of Suzu's life thereafter, and fans repeat this phrase at their 'sacred' spots.

The film also depicts Suzu living with death next door. She meets Teru, Lin's colleague, who is dying from pneumonia that she contracted after a failed suicide attempt. Sons of the neighbourhood are sent to the frontline one by one. Mothers on the home front keep their families going with meagre rations under frequent air raids. Suzu herself loses her right hand and her little niece, Harumi, during an air raid. On 6 August, Suzu, her family and friends witness an ominous pillar of cloud rising beyond the hills over Hiroshima. The atomic bomb killed tens of thousands, including Suzu's family. For ordinary people, the war ended abruptly with the emperor's radio address on 15 August. It left Suzu feeling betrayed as she thought of all the losses and sacrifices in vain. She goes to Hiroshima looking for her family, and in the barren landscape she meets Shūsaku, who has just been discharged from military duties. In the last scene, they meet a girl orphaned by the atomic bomb, and they bring her with them to her new home.

Creating authenticity

The film is based on the original manga of the same title by Kouno Fumiyo. Born in Hiroshima, Kouno has met many bomb survivors, some of whose life stories were reflected in the narrative of *In This Corner of the World*. Kouno is meticulous in her research. In the manga, fans can learn about the geography of Hiroshima and Kure, street names, wartime recipes and popular songs, the contents of rations, air-raid drills run by the *tonarigumi* (neighbourhood mutual-aid association), and what children did at school. Kouno checked, for example, the records of the day when the warship *Yamato* arrived back in Kure, which was 17 April 1944. Survivors of the war appreciated the accuracy of her depictions. Younger fans enjoy historical details that feel authentic. Fans have found her work reliable and informative, which inspired fans to dig even deeper into the world of Suzu and ordinary people's lives during the war.

When turning the static, two-dimensional visuals of the manga into a moving image, Katabuchi, like Kouno, sought authenticity (see also Chapter 17). He consulted testimonies of the local community (Nakagawa 2010) and met former residents of the Nakajima District, where the Peace Memorial Park is now. He took detailed notes of local culture and the town's atmosphere and visited archives and museums. He also consulted Moritomi Shigeo, an amateur artist who had published a book of testimonies and pencil drawings of Hiroshima during his childhood (Moritomi 2020). The bomb destroyed Moritomi's family and his home. With no surviving photographs, he drew scenes from his hometown entirely from memory. Moritomi's sketches became the basis for the film's scenes of downtown Hiroshima. In the opening scene, Suzu boards a small wooden boat and goes up one of the seven rivers of Hiroshima to the centre. She gets off at the Hiroshima Prefectural Industrial Promotion Hall (now the Atomic Bomb Dome). She crosses the Motoyasu bridge and passes Taishōya kimono shop (now the Resthouse) on the corner of Nakajimachō (Figure 16.1). Opposite the kimono shop, Suzu admires toys and caramel boxes in the shop windows. People are cheerfully enjoying the latest gossip in front of Ōtsuya Muslindō, a fashionable cloth shop. Further on, Suzu passes Hamai's barbershop where the barber and his wife are standing outside chatting with a neighbour.

Kouno's original manga does not include this episode, but Katabuchi was determined to create this scene having met survivors of the Nakajima District through the Hiroshima Fieldwork Committee. Hamai Tokusō was away at his relatives' house that day, but his parents and siblings were at home. The bomb left him an orphan. A few days after the bomb, as people searched for his family, a hand-painted porcelain dish clock was discovered in the ashes. Next to it, they found the barber's scissors and charred bones. Seven decades later, Hamai says he watches Katabuchi's film to meet his family.

Figure 16.1 The Taishōya scene from *In This Corner (and Other Corners) of the World*.
© 2019 Kouno Fumiyo, Futabasha Publishers Ltd., and the In This Corner (and Other Corners) of the World Production Committee.

Figure 16.2 Tourists visiting the Taishōya location in 2021. Author's photo.

Creating community

The story was considered to be sweet but lacking the blockbuster qualities necessary for an anime adaptation. Unable to find a sponsor, Katabuchi turned to crowdfunding. He hoped to generate 21,600,000 yen. News of the initiative spread fast through social media. The campaign ran from March to May 2015, and 2,374 supporters raised 39,121,920 yen, which easily exceeded the target. The film went on nationwide release from 12 November 2016, ran for five years, received the first Hiroshima Peace Film Award, and was the top film in the Chiketto PIA viewer satisfaction survey for 2016 ahead of the smash hit anime *Your Name* (PIA 2016). Fans' enthusiasm crossed national boundaries. The second crowdfunding effort in 2019 for screening *In This Corner (and Other Corners) of the World*, the extended version of the film, abroad gathered donations from around 3,300 people and reached 32,238,000 yen, over three times the target of 10,800,000 yen.

Fans have created a vast network and the film was screened in many theatres, big and small. Katabuchi has travelled throughout Japan visiting theatres to greet fans and give introductory talks. Communal interaction became an attraction and characteristic of viewing this film. People saw the film in groups of friends or as families. On one occasion, an atomic bomb survivor came to watch an anime film for the first time in his life. After the closing credits, he thanked the director for making the film, and the director thanked the elderly hibakusha for being there. Other cinemagoers turned out to be relatives of crew members of the warship *Yamato*, which featured in the film. The film was also shown at the theatre Hacchōza in the Fukuya department store, which Suzu sketches in the movie.

Fans and Katabuchi enjoy finding and sharing information about new and hidden associations between the details in the film and the real lives and locations that inspired it. Thus, Katabuchi's world has created an ever-expanding, intricate web of fans who enjoy being a part of and are obsessed with following the thread to see what new connection it leads them to. The more information they share, the more personal it becomes. This extended community has grown out of the fictional film *In This Corner of the World*, but members of the community find their *ibasho* (a place where they belong) in the real world.

Conclusion

Yamamura (2011: 3) states that there are three principal actors in contents tourism: creators, fans, and the local community. He defines contents tourism as 'tourism in a region or particular place that functions as media, and where tourists feel its contents (narrative quality) through their five senses. Emotive bonds are created between people, or between people and objects, through the shared narrative world' (Yamamura, 2011: 172–173). *In This Corner of the World*, therefore, exemplifies a contents tourism phenomenon.

Katabuchi, with his dedicated community of fans, local experts, and witnesses of the last war, has visually recreated the wartime civilian community with remarkable authenticity. Through the eyes of a young woman and her daily chores, we learn about wartime life. Ominously, we witness how Lin gifts Suzu a lip powder to make her look prettier in case of an air raid because, as Lin explains, even in death, 'nice-looking corpses get better treated and cleaned away before others'. We also learn that Suzu's neighbour passed by a severely burnt dying man after the atomic bomb without recognizing that he was her beloved son. The tragedy is enhanced because it sneaks into a daily routine and suddenly destroys the mundane. Therefore, KonoSeka Walkers pay homage to the *futsū* (ordinary) sites of Suzu's world and report back to their fan community where they belong. In addition to being archetypal contents tourism, the case of Suzu's world shows how the sense of *ibasho* can be a powerful motivational aspect of contents tourism.

Acknowledgements

Information in this chapter is based on interviews with: former residents of Nakajima District (including Mr Moritomi Shigeo and Mr Hamai Tokusō); Mr Nakagawa Moto'o of the Hiroshima Fieldwork Committee; Mr Ishiodori Kazunori of Aki Shobō; Ms Kikuraku Shinobu of the Hiroshima Peace Memorial Museum; the Chūgoku News; and Hiroshima City (Tourist Policy Dept.), Manager Mizuguchi; as well as the lecture given by Director Katabuchi Sunao on 6 August 2021 at Hiroshima University's Peace Project, and his interview with Professor Ochi Mitsuo, President of Hiroshima University. I am grateful to Katabuchi Sunao and Ms Kouno Fumiyo for their advice on an earlier draft of this manuscript. Ms Akita Masuzu of Genco and Ms Shirai Hitomi of Kuroburue provided the still from the film.

References

Moritomi, S. (trans. L. van der Does), 2020. *Disappeared towns, tracing memories: drawings and testimonies by Shigeo Moritomi.* Hiroshima: Hiroshima Fieldwork Committee.

Nakagawa, M., 2010. *Shōgen: kioku no naka ni ikiru machi.* Hiroshima: Hiroshima Fieldwork Committee.

PIA, 2016. *Eigakan de deguchi chōsa wo jisshi. 2016-nen eiga manzokudo rankingu 1-i wa 'Kono sekai no katasumi ni'.* PIA eiga seikatsu. https://cinema.pia.co.jp/news /168582/69306/.

Yamamura, T., 2011. *Anime, manga de chiiki shinkō: machi no fan wo umu kontentsu tsūrizumu kaihatsuhō.* Tokyo: Tōkyō Hōrei Shuppan.

17 Travelling *Grave of the Fireflies*

The gap between creators' intentions
and audiences'/tourists' interpretations

Takayoshi Yamamura

The animation film *Grave of the Fireflies* (1988) 'tells the story of a
brother and sister who lost their mother in an air raid in Kobe, and
how they both lost their lives in the ensuing hardship' (Takahata 2015:
4). It was written and directed by Takahata Isao, based on Nosaka
Akiyuki's novel of the same name. When it was decided that the original novel would be made into a film, Nosaka spoke with Takahata
about his novel as follows: '[Although the novel is …] certainly based
on my own experiences, I couldn't help glorifying the brother [Seita]
[to] make up for what I, myself, could not do in reality' (Takahata
and Nosaka 1991: 424, 426). 'I was not as kind to my sister as the
boy in the novel is, and I wrote very badly about the adults around
me, even though it was a novel' (Nosaka 1987: 270). In other words,
Nosaka constructed his literary work by fictionalizing his own war
experiences. He reconstructed them as a fictional narrative world in the
form of a *shinjū-mono*, a drama in which lovers commit double suicide
in the name of eternal love. Takahata noted that he felt like he was
reading a *shinjū-mono* by Chikamatsu Monzaemon, a jōruri and kabuki
playwright in the Edo period, when he first read the original novel
(Takahata 1991: 422).

Takahata adapted Nosaka's original novel for the animation film with
the same commitment to the faithful depiction of place and historical
fact that he had when creating the 1974 TV anime *Heidi, Girl of the Alps*
based on Johanna Spyri's original novel (Yamamura 2020). He carried
out various surveys, including location hunting, and drew on his own
war experiences. Both Nosaka and Takahata experienced the war, but
while Nosaka created a literary world through the fictionalization of his
own experiences, Takahata tried to add an element of reality to Nosaka's
fictional narrative world through the faithful representation of details of
places, things, and events. In this respect, the approaches of the two creators to their works are in sharp contrast to each other.

DOI: 10.4324/9781003239970-21

Takahata's vision can be perceived in his thorough investigation of 'everything from the structure of incendiary bombs to the flight paths of B-29s, from drop cans to phonographs' (Studio Ghibli 2013: 32). Takahata was nine years old when he 'ran for his life' from the incendiary bombs that rained down on him in Okayama, and he took great pains to depict these incendiary bombs realistically in *Grave of the Fireflies* (Takahata 1988: 74–76). Speaking about his commitment to faithfully depicting such details, Takahata argued: 'Today's dramas and films don't depict air raids properly, and I think they will become even more difficult to depict. That's what worries me. There are too many lies ... We shouldn't neglect the details' (Takahata and Kanzaki 2015: 24).

Takahata's pursuit of reality is evident in his location hunting as a contents tourist of the original novel. In March 1987, Takahata, Kondo Yoshifumi (character design, animation director), Yamamoto Nizo (art director), and Momose Yoshiyuki (layout, assistant art director) went on a location-hunting trip to places associated with Nosaka's original novel, such as Kobe city and Manchidani-cho in Nishinomiya city. At this time, Nosaka gave a guided tour to the crew based on his own war experience (Nosaka 1987: 271, Studio Ghibli 2013: 30, 42, 110).

Takahata created a realistic depiction in the film of actual buildings and landscapes, based on exhaustive location hunting. The crew took still photographs during the location hunting, and the 2012 Blu-ray edition of *Grave of the Fireflies* includes 105 of them in the special features section. Thanks to these location records and faithfully depicted scenes in the film, fans can identify the locations and travel back in time along Takahata's route. Travelogues describing *Grave of the Fireflies* contents tourism also can be found on the Internet (e.g. tati 2019; Castle n.d.). As a fan of the film and its director Takahata, I have walked the streets of Kobe and Nishinomiya with the help of these location photos, too.

Takahata insisted on faithful representation. However, he said that he did not intend to spread an anti-war message through the film. In other words, striving to improve the quality of a film is one thing, but putting messages in it is quite another. He spoke about this clearly: 'In fact, I did not make this film with the intention of conveying an anti-war message' (Takahata 1991: 441). Furthermore,

> My own experiences [of war] are strongly reflected [in this film], but I don't think that makes it an anti-war statement ... I'm a clearly anti-war person. However, it is completely different being an anti-war person and advocating anti-war stances through one's work.
>
> (Takahata and Kanzaki 2015: 24)

Nosaka, in a conversation with Takahata before the film was made, also clearly stated his desire regarding how the film should be made: 'I don't like anti-war films of any kind, and I don't like films that make the audience just feel sorry for the poor characters' (Takahata and Nosaka 1991: 426). In any case, in Takahata's words, the film *Grave of the Fireflies* is also, as Nosaka intended in his original novel, 'a kind of *shinjū-mono*, the first since Chikamatsu's work' from the Edo era, in which 'the premise of death' and the drama of 'how it happened is expressed in a condensed form by a brother and sister alone' (Takahata and Kanzaki 2015: 24).

However, after the film's release, Takahata learned that 'an overwhelming majority of people who saw the film read an "anti-war" message into the film' and that 'there was a simple but honest response across the country such as "we must never start a war again"' (Takahata 1991: 443–444). Similar reactions by contents tourists of the film can be seen in their online feedback. For example, one fan, after visiting the locations, wrote in his blog: 'I will continue to convey the horror and stupidity of war to the world ... I hope that this article will inspire you to visit the locations and learn more about the war, even if only a little' (tati 2019). In response to such audience reactions, Takahata said he noticed that 'it is a natural reaction' for many people to 'accept the film as an anti-war film'. He 'regretted his previous thinking' (Takahata 1991: 444) that 'he had been uncomfortable with the film being placed in the anti-war genre' insisting that 'it is not an anti-war film' (Takahata 2015: 4).

Here, the creator's intention and the audience's interpretation are two different things. In light of the above, it is suggested that even without the creator's anti-war message his realistic portrayal of the locations, firebombs, and other elements of his narrative world resulted in a spontaneous anti-war interpretation by the audience.

In 2020, 33 years after the location hunting, a monument inscribed with 'birthplace of the novel *Grave of the Fireflies*' was erected in Nishinomiya Earthquake Memorial Park, Manchidani-cho, Nishinomiya city, to mark the area where Nosaka's original novel *Grave of the Fireflies* was set (Figure 17.1). The planning committee, comprising local residents and fans of Nosaka, collected donations to pay for it. There is a slate next to the monument titled 'Nosaka Akiyuki's war experience', with an explanation about the original novel and a picture of Seita and Setsuko from the anime movie poster. It is the latest contents tourist destination for the narrative world of *Grave of the Fireflies*, both the original novel and the animation film.

On the back of this monument are carved the following words: 'In this place where Nosaka's novel is set, seventy-five years after the end of the war we still pass on the horrors of war and pray for lasting peace for

Figure 17.1 The monument at the birthplace of the novel *Grave of the Fireflies*, Nishinomiya. Author's photo.

the children of today and the future' (author's translation). Furthermore, the fact that the monument was constructed in Nishinomiya Earthquake Memorial Park, a place of remembrance for those who died in the Great Hanshin-Awaji Earthquake (17 January 1995), is significant in that the local community has placed the monument in a place for mourning the dead.

Interestingly, neither the inscriptions at the site, nor the explanatory panels, nor the monument's commemorative journal edited by the committee (Hotaru no Haka Kinenhi Kenpi Jikkō Iinkai 2020) mention the fact that the original novel and animation film was a *shinjū-mono*. The contents are presented almost exclusively in an anti-war context. The gap (which is mediated by the contents) between the creators, who aim purely to produce a work of art or entertainment, and the interpretations by audiences and the contents tourists who consume it, likely can be seen in all contents. However, as far as war-related contents are concerned, these gaps raise various sensitive issues related to historical awareness and political ideas. Therefore, the intentions of these creators of war-related contents and the literary and interpretive structures of the audiences and contents tourists remain unclear. This is one of the main issues that we have aimed to address in this book.

References

Castle, n.d. *Hotaru no haka*. Ghibli furīku. http://www.ghibli-freak.net/hotaru/location1.html.

Hotaru no Haka Kinenhi Kenpi Jikkō Iinkai, 2020. *Shōsetsu Hotaru no haka tanjō no chi*. Nishinomiya: Hotaru no Haka Kinenhi Kenpi Jikkō Īnkai.

Nosaka, A., 1987. Anime osorubeshi. *Shosetsu shincho*, 41 (9) (519), 270–271.

Studio Ghibli, 2013. Studio Ghibli monogatari: *Hotaru no haka* hen. In: Studio Ghibli and Bunshun Bunko, eds. *Ghibli no kyōkasho 4 Hotaru no haka*. Tokyo: Bungei Shunju, 23–36.

Takahata, I., 1988. 'Molotov no pan-kago' no nazo. *Ushio*, 350, 74–76.

Takahata, I., 1991. *Eiga wo tsukurinagara kangaeta koto*. Tokyo: Tokuma Shoten.

Takahata, I., 2015. *Kimi ga sensō wo hosshinai naraba*. Tokyo: Iwanami Shoten.

Takahata, I. and Kanzaki, N., 2015. Anime sakka no manazashi. *Mahora*, 83, 22–28.

Takahata, I. and Nosaka, A., 1991. Seita to Setsuko no mita 8-gatsu 15-nichi no sora to umi wa kono ue naku kirei datta. In: I. Takahata, ed. *Eiga wo tsukurinagara kangaeta koto*. Tokyo: Tokuma Shoten, 421–428.

tati, 2019. *Hotaru no haka no naka ni aru 'hitode nashi' (saihenshū-ban): roke-chi junrei*. 15 August. Goo blog. https://blog.goo.ne.jp/sasuraieigabito/e/3bdd12532a826ab204adf9d865aaa3d8.

Yamamura, T., 2020. Travelling *Heidi*: international contents tourism induced by Japanese anime. In: T. Yamamura and P. Seaton, eds. *Contents tourism and pop culture fandom: transnational tourist experiences*. Bristol: Channel View Publications, 62–81.

18 Tours of Tokkōtai (kamikaze) training bases

Luli van der Does

Towards the end of the Pacific War, the Allied fleet in the Pacific faced an onslaught of suicide attacks by pilots of the Imperial Japanese Forces. The Allies named both the attacks and the pilots the Kamikaze ('divine wind'), but the Japanese official term is Tokubetsu kōgeki tai (Special Attack Corps), abbreviated as Tokkōtai. Kamikaze is also a term in Shintoist literature alluding to the legend of the thirteenth-century battles during the Mongol invasion of Japan (Chapter 3). Kublai Khan's formidable fleet attacked the coastal areas of northern Kyushu, outnumbering the Japanese by ten to one. Defeat was inevitable against the Mongols' technological (gunpowder weapons) and numerical superiority. The Japanese fought in suicidal defence, but a sudden storm sank the Mongol ships. Miraculously, the divine wind saved the Japanese. The historical accuracy of this story is debatable, but the legend of self-sacrificial bravery and divine intervention became established in Japanese popular culture. The myth was resurrected in 1944–1945 to justify suicide tactics against the Allied fleet.

The Kyushu region has a high concentration of memorial sites to Tokkōtai that continue to draw tourists of all generations. As raw memories of the brutality of war fade with time, a 'kamikaze world', a tourism imaginary commoditizing the Tokkōtai, has emerged (Seaton 2019). The Chiran Peace Museum is the main site, and there are lower-key sites at museums in Tachiarai and Bansei, but the same narrative of kamikaze courage and self-sacrifice drives contents tourism at these sites dedicated to the memories of Imperial Army Tokkōtai. However, this chapter focuses on four former Imperial Navy Tokkōtai training bases: Kanoya, Kushira, Izumi, and Usa.

Kanoya

Our tour of naval Tokkōtai sites begins at Kanoya Air Base Museum, annexed to the Kanoya Air Field of Japan's Maritime Self-Defense Force

DOI: 10.4324/9781003239970-22

(JMSDF). The museum presents Japanese aviation history, technical development, and the political, economic, strategic, and psychological factors that drove Imperial Japan to use the Tokkō (special attack) strategy. The Kanoya base opened in 1936, a year before the Kanoya Conference, where the plans for the Pearl Harbor attack were discussed. As the war intensified, the Fifth Air Fleet Command was established in February 1945. Over 800 airmen took off from Kanoya base in Operation Kikusui (Chrysanthemum Water), a series of ten concerted aerial attacks during the Battle of Okinawa between 6 April and 22 June 1945. On average, the pilots were 19 years old and had minimum aviation experience (van der Does-Ishikawa 2015), making Kanoya a particularly poignant war memorial destination.

Operation Kikusui was the backdrop for Hyakuta Naoki's million-selling novel *Eien no Zero* (*The Eternal Zero*) and the 2013 blockbuster film of the same title. The film courted domestic and international controversy about whether it reflected ultra-nationalistic views on war history (Suzuki 2015). Meanwhile, many filmgoers enjoyed the human drama of unsung heroes, who were misunderstood by people but bonded by brotherly love, engaging in suicide attacks against massively superior enemy forces to protect their compatriots. This narrative template echoes the legend of the Mongol invasion in Kyushu. Historians, film critics, and fans have also compared the Tokkō narrative to Leonidas the Spartan king and his 300 men at the Battle of Thermopylae (Rebenich 2002: 327). The audience may also project their own emotional experiences of life's injustices, such as those stemming from the sacrificial work ethic in today's corporate culture, onto the unfortunate pilots (Sōtome n.d.), rather than glorify the war and Kamikaze attacks per se.

Kushira

Twelve kilometres northeast of Kanoya is the former Kushira Airfield, established in April 1944. Approximately 5,000 Naval Aviator Preparatory Course Trainees, or *yokaren*, trained there in aviation mechanics, manoeuvres, and telecommunications. As the war intensified, training units were attached to operational units and, from March 1945, converted into a Special Attack Corps. A total of 363 Tokkō pilots and 210 other fighter pilots took off from Kushira Base, never to return. The underground telecommunications bunker at the airfield is seven metres deep and 57 metres long. Visitors descend a narrow staircase down to the telecommunications room. Tokkō pilots sent their last Morse code signal here before their attack. When transmission stopped, it meant another life was lost. The tours of Kushira and Kanoya airfields present many stories of individual pilots as well as operational details. They form a part of the recommended local itinerary provided by the municipal tourism association located at the entrance of the Kanoya JMSDF base.

Izumi

By contrast, Tokkōtai-related historical sites in Izumi are still largely left untouched or protected by volunteers. Izumi Naval Air Field opened in 1940 as a supplemental aerodrome for Kanoya and Omura. On 15 April 1943, it was annexed to the Twelfth Joint Air Corps and began training young recruits. B29 raids intensified from April 1945 during the Battle of Okinawa, when the operation unit Ginga was stationed at Izumi. Japan had exhausted its supplies of airworthy planes, trained pilots, and fuel by the summer of 1945 and resorted to sending off under-skilled teenage pilots in trainer aircraft with one-way's worth of fuel to defend the country. They took off day after day on Tokkō missions, resulting in over 260 deaths.

Long straight roads crisscross the city. They are remnants of the former runways. The ruins of *entaigō* (semi-circular bunkers) stand beside the roads. A mound in a park hides the entrance to an underground operations centre. Paper cranes on strings, Tokkō pilots' poetry, and records of their missions are exhibited inside. Across from the park stands Tokkō Shrine, which was established in 1943 as a guardian shrine for pilots and later became a place of commemoration for Tokkōtai pilots. In the shrine grounds, the *Nanpō no Kanata* (Beyond the South Seas) statue of a youthful Tokkō pilot gazes towards the south seas. It is dedicated to Seki Yukio, Kanazashi Isao, and every airman who perished in Tokkō operations. Kanazashi took off from Izumi on 19 March 1945 and hit the Essex-class aircraft carrier USS Franklin off Cape Ashizuri. He had been inspired by the first kamikaze pilot, Seki Yukio, whose special attack mission was during the Battle of Leyte Gulf in October 1944. The Allies had cut the Japanese supply lines and destroyed most carrier-borne and land-based aircraft as well as naval vessels. Faced with the impending US invasion of the Philippines, inspiration was sought from ancient heroes. Admiral Onishi Takijiro issued the first order. On 25 October, Lieutenant Seki led five Zero fighters in the first Shimpu (Divine Wind) attack. Seki crash-dived his plane into the USS St. Lo and sunk it. Seki's sacrifice evoked the legend of the Divine Wind against the Mongol invasion and inspired many more to follow.

However, Seki reportedly confided with a journalist that he believed the suicidal attack order was a sign of Japan's desperation and inevitable defeat. He would obey the order 'not for the Empire, but only to protect my wife and loved ones from the Yankees' (Onoda 1971). Seki's words were published after the war, adding to his popularity. Admirers saw them as a symbol of defiance against the injustice of war and institutional society. This reveals the contested interpretations of the kamikaze: while many eulogize their patriotism and sacrifice, others admire Tokkōtai pilots as emblems of anti-war expression, and others can see the potential of using the sites as a testimonial heritage of war.[1]

Usa

On 1 October 1939, a facility of the Imperial Navy Air Service under the command of Kure Naval District was established in Usa. It was a combat training base for the crew of carrier-borne attack aircraft and bombers and occupied 184 hectares. A special attack Ohka (glider bomber) squadron Jinrai came from Miyazaki to train at Usa before moving to Kanoya. The Allies frequently conducted air raids in March and April 1945, resulting in several hundred military and civilian casualties. Therefore, Usa's community is committed to preserving the town's war sites to let them 'speak of horrors of war and human suffering' (Oita Heritage 2017). Local historians and the city's education board have jointly campaigned for the conservation of ten remaining bunkers. Over the years, the airfield was converted back to agricultural fields, and the runway was turned into public roads, but visitors can still feel its sheer size. Ruins are scattered over a vast area: a parachute storage building with bullet holes in the walls, water management facilities, and other remnants of the airbase. They form a part of an open-air museum, while a small building on the southside of the airfield houses a full-scale model of a Zero fighter and an Ohka. Damaged propellers and a claustrophobic cockpit (Figure 18.1) testify to the fragility of life in futile missions, inducing one visitor to write sensory reflections on Usa's local history on TripAdvisor (Rokai 2015).

Conclusions

Tokkōtai-related tourism exemplifies a 'usable narrative world' (Figure 1.3) at the overlap of the three tourism imaginaries discussed in Chapter 1: (subjective) war experience, (objective) war heritage, and war-related entertainment. Packaged in an emotive formula with ancient and universal roots, the enduring narratives of self-sacrifice can cater to tourists' emotional consumption of the spaces once occupied by their tragic heroes. Initially, the semi-fictionalized human dramas depicted in numerous works of entertainment such as *The Eternal Zero* inspire them

Figure 18.1 A reconstructed cockpit at a museum on the site of the former Usa Airfield. Author's photos.

to visit these sites as light-hearted contents tourists. One such tourist visited Kanoya 'out of curiosity' after seeing Tokkōtai dramas and films, but once there, the suicidal mission of the people of 'my son's age' hit home. Now she considers the site a must-see (Dānei 2014). Another visitor noted how reflecting 'in situ' can trigger a critical examination of the narrative of 'legendary courage and self-sacrifice' (2008sannohfighters 2020). When thus inspired, tourists can go further down the heritage trail, tracing the path of Tokkōtai trainees in Kanoya, Kushira, Izumi, Usa, and beyond.

Note

1 Interview with Mr Inoue Haruhiro, Department of Social Education (Cultural Heritage), Usa city and Usa Peace Museum.

References

2008sannohfighters, 2020. *Kangaesaserareru naiyō desu.* Trip Advisor. https://www .tripadvisor.jp/ShowUserReviews-g1023440-d8313570-r738622948-Usa_City _Peace_Museum-Usa_Oita_Prefecture_Kyushu.html.
Dānei, 2014. *Ichido otozureru kachi ari to omoimasu.* Trip Advisor. https://www .tripadvisor.jp/ShowUserReviews-g1022923-d2102824-r230202885-Kanoya _Air_Base_Museum-Kanoya_Kagoshima_Prefecture_Kyushu.html.

Oita Heritage, 2017. Ruins of Usa Imperial Japanese Navy Air Service battlefield. *Oita Heritage*. http://oitaisan.com/english/heritage/ruins-of-usa-imperial-japanese-navy-air-service-battlefield/.

Onoda, M., 1971. Kaisōroku: Shimpu-Tokkōtai shutsugeki-no-hi. *In*: Kyō no wadai sha, eds. *Taiheiyō sensō dokyumentarī*, Vol. 23. Tokyo: Kyō no wadai sha, 10–19.

Rebenich, S., 2002. From Thermopylae to Stalingrad: the myth of Leonidas in German historiography. *In*: A. Powerll and S. Hodkinson, eds. *Sparta, beyond the mirage*. London: Classical Press of Wales, 323–349.

Rokai, 2015. *Usa ni kitara zehi otozurete itadakitai supotto*. Trip Advisor. https://www.tripadvisor.jp/ShowUserReviews-g1023440-d8313570-r280583864-Usa_City_Peace_Museum-Usa_Oita_Prefecture_Kyushu.html.

Seaton, P., 2019. Kamikaze museums and contents tourism. *Journal of War & Culture Studies*, 12 (1), 67–84.

Sōtome, N., n.d. *Kōkami Shōji ga kaita Tokkotai-in no jinsei wo saguru*. MOC Moment of Choice. https://moc.style/world/interview-playwright-kokamishoji-01/.

Suzuki, S., 2015. Nationalism lite? The commodification of non-Japanese speech in Japanese media. *Japanese Language and Literature*, 49 (2), 509–529.

van der Does-Ishikawa, L., 2015. Contested memories of the Kamikaze and the self-representations of Tokkō-tai youth in their missives home. *Japan Forum*, 27 (3), 345–379.

19 Repatriation and the *enka* ballad *Ganpeki no haha*

Akiko Sugawa-Shimada

Ganpeki no haha (Mother on the quay) was a hit song in the 1950s and 1970s about the Siberia internment.[1] The lyrics are based on the actual story of a mother of an unrepatriated soldier, Ise Hashino, who commuted from Tokyo to Maizuru port in Kyoto prefecture to wait for the repatriation of her only son Shinji after the Second World War. Ise believed him to be alive, even after receiving notification of his death in action in 1954. She kept searching for him until she died aged 81 in 1981. In 2000, Shinji was found alive. He had a family with his Chinese wife in Shanghai. Ise's wish was half granted: her son was alive. But Shinji decided not to return to Japan because he did not want to damage people's admiration for his mother (Osada 2015: 753–4).

Six days before Japan's surrender, on 9 August 1945, the Soviet army invaded Manchuria, and thereafter Karafuto and the Kurile Islands, too. They captured approximately 575,000 Japanese soldiers and civilians, who were sent to concentration camps and forced to work in Siberia and other parts of central Asia for several years (Maizuru Repatriation Memorial Museum n.d.). Approximately 473,000 were eventually repatriated, but 55,000 died of forced labour, cold, and hunger during their internment (Ministry of Health, Labour and Welfare 2009). Maizuru port was one of eighteen ports for repatriation in Japan set up in 1945. The first repatriation ship from Nakhodka arrived in Maizuru in 1950. Maizuru was also the final repatriation port open until 1958.

Having heard that Shinji was captured by the Soviet army in Manchuria and sent to Siberia, Ise went to Maizuru from Tokyo every time a repatriation ship arrived. When Shinji did not disembark, she stood on the quay in despair for a long time. Her story was reported on NHK radio news in 1954, which inspired poet Fujita Masato to write lyrics about her. Hirakawa Namiryu set the lyrics to music. *Ganpeki no haha* was so touching that enka singer Kikuchi Akiko welled up in tears when she recorded the song at Teichiku Record Co. Ltd. (Osada 2015: 753–4).

DOI: 10.4324/9781003239970-23

Nevertheless, her rendition of *Ganpeki no haha* with three verses was an instant success in 1954.

Even before *Ganpeki no haha*, another song about the Siberia internment, *Ikoku no oka* (Hills in a foreign country), had already been a hit in 1948. This song was originally composed by Yoshida Tadashi, a soldier in Manchuria in 1943, as propaganda music for military exercises. It was called *Daikōanrei toppa enshū no uta* (Training to charge the Daxinganling mountains). Masuda Kōji, a soldier interned in Vladivostok, put lyrics to Yoshida's music to cheer up his fellow internees. It was often sung among Japanese internees in Soviet camps because it depicted male friendship between war comrades trying to overcome hardship during their internment. The song became well known to the Japanese public when Nakamura Kōzō, a soldier repatriated from Siberia, sang it on the NHK radio programme *Nodo jiman* (an amateur singing contest) in 1948 (Wajima 2010: 88). After he finished singing, he said that there were still so many Japanese prisoners of war left behind in Siberia (Tsubotani 2005). The song was renamed *Ikoku no oka* and sung by Nakamura and a professional singer, Takeyama Itsurō. It was also adapted into a movie of the same title in 1949. Yoshida and Masuda were repatriated to Japan in 1948 and 1950, respectively, oblivious to how much popularity their song had gained in Japan.

Ikoku no oka is a song about the Siberian internment from the viewpoint of prisoners of war. Since it is a song in two beats to rouse and encourage, it is similar to military songs. However, Kikuchi's song *Ganpeki no haha* was a sentimental, anti-war popular song about the tragedy caused by war and a mother's love for her son. At that time, repatriated soldiers and civilians were a familiar presence in Japanese people's lives via news reports. There were many one-legged or one-armed soldiers begging for money on the street. However, as people's war memories faded amidst their embracement of rapid economic growth in the 1960s, the popularity of *Ganpeki no haha* gradually subsided.

But in 1972 *Ganpeki no haha* was revived and became a three-million-sales hit when it was arranged in a *rōkyoku* style. It was sung by Futaba Yuriko, who had a *rōkyoku* career before entering show business. *Rōkyoku*, or *naniwabushi*, is a Japanese traditional style of narrative singing with a shamisen[2] that emerged in the early twentieth century. *Rōkyoku* usually recounts a sad story, so the *rōkyoku* style matched the theme of *Ganpeki no haha*. There were emotional monologues by Muromachi Kyonosuke included within the song, and Futaba sang *Ganpeki no haha* as if she was a mother talking to her missing son.

There are three monologues between the three verses, and the final one pleads to the wind to tell Shinji that her mother has been standing for a long time on the quayside waiting for him (Osada 2015: 753). Futaba's singing style was later categorized as modern *enka*, namely Japanese sentimental ballad music but with distinctive jazz and rockabilly elements from foreign music (Wajima 2010: 76). Unlike Kikuchi's 1954 rendition, Futaba's *Ganpeki no haha* was no longer seen as an anti-war song. Instead, the mother's love in this song represented idealized traditional motherhood at a time when motherly love was in a perceived crisis. In the 1970s, a crisis of motherhood became a serious social issue, fuelled by sensationalized stories of newborn babies being abandoned in coin lockers in Tokyo (Ohinata 2016: n.p.). In male-centred Japanese society, child-rearing is traditionally regarded as a mother's job. In the 1970s, many young women worked longer and delayed marriage. On one hand, the mass media welcomed the change as the emancipation of women, but on the other hand, they criticized such women as unwomanly. Within this patriarchal social context, *Ganpeki no haha* evoked nostalgia for traditional motherhood ideals (Osada 2015: 754). The story was adapted into a movie in 1976 and a TV drama in the following year, both of the same title. Futaba retired in 2011, but the song has been sung by many popular female *enka* singers since, such as Sakamoto Fuyumi, one of Futaba's apprentices.

In April 1988, the Maizuru Repatriation Memorial Museum was opened. It contains exhibitions of Ise Hashino's letters to her son, the soundtracks of *Ganpeki no haha* by Kikuchi and Futaba and of *Ikoku no oka*, and materials that tell of the harshness of life during the Siberian internment. In October 2015, 570 items out of its extensive collection of materials were registered as part of the UNESCO Memory of the World Programme (Maizuru Repatriation Memorial Museum 2015; Bull and Ivings 2019).

The restored Maizuru pier bridge is approximately a 20-minute walk away from the museum. The museum and the pier bridge are popular destinations for tourists. Inside the museum, visitors can imagine life in the concentration camps by entering a life-size model room. When you enter the small dark room, you can see five mannequins of Japanese prisoners of war in shabby coats talking about how cold it is. You can hear a howling wind and the window is covered with snow because the heater in the centre of the room only has a little fire. In another section, you can see five mannequin prisoners with downcast eyes eating a thin slice of bread with a small amount of watery soup. In the exhibition area, materials that show life in the Siberian camps are presented in glass showcases: repatriated soldiers' bags, boots, clothes, and the 'Birch tree diary', a diary of a prisoner in Siberia written on birch tree bark, which was registered as part of the UNESCO Memory of the World Programme.

Figure 19.1 The restored pier of Maizuru repatriation port. The bell of mourning was donated by Maizuru National Society of Friends Commemorating Repatriation (Hikiage wo kinen suru Maizuru zenkoku tomo no kai). Author's photo.

Behind the museum building on a hill is the Repatriation Memorial Park, where monuments to the songs *Ikoku no oka* and *Ganpeki no haha* stand, along with a cenotaph. There is a cozy roofed rest space, from which you can see beautiful Maizuru Bay. Although the exhibition is depressing, the café and souvenir shop in the museum and the Repatriation Memorial Park seem to be sites for local retirees and the elderly to gather. When I visited in 2020, a large group of elderly people wearing masks were enjoying a chat over lunch in the museum café, despite the COVID-19 pandemic. In the entrance hall, there were some flyers about events for interactions among citizens at the museum. Repatriation has become part of local heritage, and the tourist sites commemorating this history help bring the local community together. As an example of war-related contents tourism, however, Maizuru shows how popular culture enhances the narrative quality of an otherwise bleak site of remembrance and gives it relevance and appeal to subsequent generations, too.

Notes

1 The song and lyrics are available online at: https://www.uta-net.com/movie /21012/
2 Shamisen is a three-stringed Japanese traditional musical instrument.

References

Bull, J. and Ivings, S., 2019. Return on display: memories of postcolonial migration at Maizuru. *Japan Forum*, 31 (3), 336–357.

Maizuru Repatriation Memorial Museum, n.d. *Shiberia yokuryū*. Maizuru Repatriation Memorial Museum. https://m-hikiage-museum.jp/education/siberia.html.

Maizuru Repatriation Memorial Museum, 2015. *Maizuru e no seikan. 1945–1956 Shiberia yokuryū tō Nihonjin no hongoku e no hikiage no kiroku.* Maizuru Repatriation Memorial Museum. https://m-hikiage-museum.jp/contents/?cat=3.

Ministry of Health, Labour and Welfare, 2009. *Siberia yokuryū chū shibōsha ni kansuru shiryō no chōsa ni tsuite.* Ministry of Health, Labour and Welfare. https://www.mhlw.go.jp/seisaku/2009/11/01.html.

Ohinata, M., 2016. *Zōho boseiai shinwa no wana.* Tokyo: Nihon hyōronsha (Kindle version).

Osada, G., 2015. *Sensō ga nokoshita uta: uta ga akasu sensō no haikei.* Tokyo: Zen Ongaku Shuppansha.

Tsubotani, H., 2005. 'Ikoku no oka' hikiage. *Asahi shinbun*, Yamagata edition. 3 August, p. 27.

Wajima, Y., 2010. *Tsukurareta 'nihon no kokoro' shinwa: Enka wo meguru sengo taishū ongaku shi.* Tokyo: Kōbunsha.

Part V

Postwar Japan

20 *Kantai Collection* and entertainmentization of the Second World War

Kyungjae Jang

Defeat in the Second World War acted as a kind of memory resetting device in Japan as militarism gave way to narratives of peace and 'not repeating the mistakes of the past'. However, some places in Japan still preserve and pass on military heritage. This includes the four naval port cities of Kure, Yokosuka, Sasebo, and Maizuru, which were involved in postwar geopolitics in the Asia–Pacific region, and in particular, played a military role during the Korean War. These naval cities generate a contradiction within their postwar memories: on the one hand, they express the Japanese mantra of peace (disconnection with the wartime past), but as active naval cities today they host military forces with the capability to threaten peace (Uesugi 2012; 2014).

Meanwhile, in East Asia since the 2010s, particularly in the worlds of manga, anime, and games, there has been a boom in popular culture contents featuring weapons (see also Chapter 8), and particularly Second World War weapons. *Girls und Panzer* (2012), for example, has high school girls racing Second World War tanks around Ōarai town in Ibaraki prefecture. This triggered both significant contents tourism and controversy due to the collaboration of the Japan Self-Defense Force in some fan events (Yamamura 2019: 13–15). Other contents feature anthropomorphisms of weaponry, particularly weapons personified as *shōjo* (young girls – see Sugawa 2019: 56). Recent examples include the game *Kantai Collection* (2013), featuring anthropomorphisms of Imperial Japanese Navy ships called *kanmusu* ('ship girls'), and *Shooting Girl* (2015), a similar game to *Kantai Collection* but with anthropomorphisms of guns. In such narrative worlds, fans tend to be attracted to the characters rather than a specific storyline or world view, a phenomenon that Azuma Hiroki (2001) called 'animalization' and 'database consumption'.

Fans, local people, and the Japan Self-Defense Force (SDF) consume or utilize these contents in different ways and for varying motives, but all activities connect back to war memories. Fans visit places that appear in

DOI: 10.4324/9781003239970-25

the contents for two main purposes. Some fans are interested in the war history and visit associated places, while other fans separate the characters from war history and visit places most connected to the characters in the works of entertainment. Local people cooperate with production companies to hold contents-related events with the aim of attracting new forms of tourism, although for some the use of the contents might be considered a 'cushion' that softens the passing down of military heritage in a country where the rhetoric of peace is strongly engrained in public discourse. The SDF, meanwhile, can use the popularity of contents to help with public relations (Chapter 22; Yamamura 2019). This chapter explores how war-related contents connect to memories of the Second World War, and how entertainment contents are consumed by fans, regions, and the SDF in naval port cities through the case of *Kantai Collection*.

Kantai Collection ('Fleet Collection', hereafter '*KanColle*') is an online PC browser game based on Japanese Imperial Navy warships released in April 2013. It was later adapted into a TV animation and film. In the game the player becomes an 'admiral', collects *kanmusu*, and fights against the fictional 'abyssal fleet'. As the game's name suggests, the ultimate goal is to collect rare warships rather than win battles. Although it is not made available in East Asia other than in Japan (as it deals with weapons from the Second World War), many Chinese, Korean, and Taiwanese fans use VPN to play *KanColle*. They even hold events and visit related places in Japan and their home countries.

A distinctive feature of *KanColle*-induced tourism is the displacement of war memories at commemorative sites via casual consumption, or the non-contextual consumption of war-related places. An example is *KanColle* fans' visits to the memorial to the crew of the Japanese cruiser *Naka*, whose name comes from a river in Ibaraki prefecture. *Naka* was sunk by US forces in 1944 with the loss of 240 crew members. There is *chūkonhi* memorial (lit. 'monument for loyal souls') for the dead in Ōarai Isosaki Shrine, which is close to the mouth of the Naka river. However, in *KanColle* the character Naka is not a particularly good ship to receive during the in-game lottery when players collect a ship. This gave rise to a saying among fans, 'I quit being a fan of *Naka*' (*Naka no fan wo yamemasu*). However, this aspect of fan behaviour did not just stay within online fan communities. In 2013, some *KanColle* fans went to Ōarai Isosaki Shrine, drew a picture of the character *Naka* on an *ema* (a votive plaque for making a wish at a shrine), and said that they had quit being a fan of hers. The shrine is an actual memorial to the crew of the real ship *Naka* and is visited by bereaved relatives of the crew. Word of this incident spread on social media, and while there were no responses from the bereaved families, the fan community demanded that the game be separated from reality. A similar incident happened in Kure in January 2019. Some *KanColle* fans visited the Kure Former Naval Cemetery (Nagasako Park) and put *KanColle* character cards on almost every monument to warships, including the memorial for the crew of the battleship *Yamato*. This behaviour was also heavily criticized on social media.

Meanwhile, local residents, especially in former naval districts, have used *KanColle* as a means of attracting new tourists to the region by collaborating with the production companies. In 2019, Kure city in Hiroshima prefecture and Sasebo city in Nagasaki prefecture held events called '130th Kure 2019' and '130th Sasebo 2019' to commemorate the 130th anniversaries of both cities establishing naval bases during the Meiji period. However, the events were not aimed at the general public, but rather *KanColle* fans. In Kure, there were dances held on two evenings, special live performances by voice actresses, a stamp rally, joint events held with the Yamato Museum and Irifuneyama Memorial, and local restaurants collaborated in the event, too. In Sasebo, cardboard cutouts and images from the anime were placed in the airport, harbour, and around the city, and many people were seen having their pictures taken by them (Sazanami Kaihen 2020). Game-related goods were sold in both cities. At the Sasebo Citizens' Culture Hall (Former Sasebo Naval District Triumphal Memorial Hall), young women dressed in character costumes gave live performances of *taiko* drumming. Interestingly, in both cities, there were no other official events to commemorate the 130th anniversaries of the naval districts, and these game-related events were the only official events held in which the cities were involved.

The third actor is the Japan Maritime Self-Defense Force (JMSDF), which holds various public relations events to promote JMSDF. Some have involved collaborations with *KanColle*. Like many other countries' navies, JMSDF often names its modern ships using the names of ships from earlier periods of naval history. Consequently, JMSDF promotional events can include vessels bearing the same names as the old Imperial Japanese Navy ships that appear in *KanColle*. One example is the Aegis destroyer *Kongō*, which shares its name with a character in *KanColle*. On 27 April 2019, a special public event for cosplayers was held at Shimonoseki port, where *Kongō* was anchored for three days (Figure 20.1). One of the public events was a special event for cosplayers only, organized by the Self-Defense Forces Yamaguchi Regional Cooperation Headquarters in collaboration with the local cosplay event organizer COSMAI. I participated in this event. An SDF officer guided us around the ships, and for an hour there was a photo shoot event. It was possible to take photos without restrictions on the bridge and the

Figure 20.1 A cosplayer dressed as a *kanmusu* ('ship girl') at a JMSDF public relations
event. Author's photo.

front and rear decks, where fans most wanted to take photos. I was one
of about 20 cosplayers and photographers who participated, and participants' costumes were mostly of *KanColle* characters.

This chapter has explored some of the ways in which fans, local communities, and the Japan Self-Defense Force are consuming and utilizing
contents such as *KanColle,* and the connections to actual memories of the
Second World War. The examples of fans leaving *ema* or game cards at
actual naval memorial sites in Ōarai and Kure indicate the tensions that
can arise when pop culture fans on a 'sacred site pilgrimage' consume
monuments commemorating the war dead when wartime comrades and
bereaved relatives are still alive. This shines a light on the limitations of
entertainmentization of wars within living memory. Although the contents that fans are consuming are fictionalized, they are still connected to
actual historical events. If the war becomes decontextualized via entertainmentization, fans and survivors may form very different 'interpretive
communities' (Chapter 1) with the potential for significant misunderstandings as they visit the same war-related sites for very different purposes. Furthermore, the involvement of local governments and the SDF

in fan events raises important questions about the ways in which contents-related events can act as a 'cushion' in the process of passing down memories of war and military heritage. Do such events simply constitute local people's desires to take commercial or other advantage of fans' visits as contents tourists to their communities, or is there a deeper agenda, namely the use of entertainment contents as a smokescreen masking the promotion of a particular political agenda? This is a question Yamamura (2019) has noted for other similar cases of SDF collaborations with anime producers. The case of *KanColle* provides, therefore, a microcosm of the tensions and contestations at the intersections of war memories and war-related entertainment, consumption and commemoration, and remembering and forgetting.

References

Azuma, H., 2001. *Otaku: Japan's database animals.* Minneapolis: University of Minnesota Press.

Sazanami Kaihen, 2020. *Shingata koronauirusu de Kankore chinjufu meguri no Sasebo wa dō natta no ka.* Sazanami Kaihen. https://sazanami.net/20200314-kancolle-sasebo-naval-district-130th/.

Sugawa, A., 2019. Playing with militarism in/with *Arpeggio* and *Kantai Collection*: effects of *shōjo* images in war-related contents tourism in Japan. *Journal of War & Culture Studies*, 12 (1), 53–66.

Uesugi, K., 2012. Renzoku to danzetsu no toshizō: mō hitotsu no 'heiwa' toshi Kure. *In*: Y. Fukuma, M. Yamaguchi, and K. Yoshimura, eds. *Fukusū no Hiroshima: kioku no sengo-shi to media no rikigaku.* Tokyo: Seikyusha, 103–138.

Uesugi, K., 2014. Gunkō toshi 'Kure' kara heiwa sangyō kōwan toshi 'Kure' e. *In*: Y. Sakane, ed. *Chiiki no naka no guntai 5: nishi no guntai to gunkō toshi Chūgoku Shikoku.* Tokyo: Yoshikawa kōbunkan, 104–130.

Yamamura, T., 2019. Cooperation between anime producers and the Japan self-defense force: creating fantasy and/or propaganda? *Journal of War & Culture Studies*, 12 (1), 8–23.

21 The war metaphors underpinning Mizuki Shigeru yōkai tourism

Qiaodan Wang and Philip Seaton

Mizuki Shigeru (1922–2015) is one of Japan's most celebrated manga artists for his works set in the fantasy world of yōkai (monsters or ghosts in Japanese folklore). His most famous character is Kitarō, the protagonist of works such as *Gegege no Kitarō*, and many of Mizuki's works have been translated into English. As part of an economic revitalization project in his hometown of Sakaiminato, Tottori prefecture, the Mizuki Shigeru Road opened in 1993. In 2021, 177 bronze yōkai statues lined the 800 metres from Sakaiminato Station to the Mizuki Shigeru Museum, which was opened in 2003 (Mizuki Shigeru Museum n.d.). Its success as a tourist site made Mizuki Shigeru Road an important early case study within contents tourism research (Masubuchi 2010: 91–110; Yamamura 2011: 11–19) and helped popularize the more general phenomenon of yōkai tourism (Myoki 2020: 99–100). In 2010, NHK's morning drama was based on an autobiography penned by Mizuki's wife, Mura Nunoe. *Gegege no nyōbō* (Gegege's Wife) also triggered considerable contents tourism as part of the widely recognized phenomenon of *asadora* ('morning drama') tourism (Scherer and Thelen 2020; Chōfu-shi Kankō Kyōkai 2017). Much of this tourism was to Chōfu, the city in western Tokyo where he lived from 1959 to his death, and which is the other main 'sacred site' of Mizuki Shigeru contents tourism. Mizuki died in 2015, but his popularity has not waned. Tourism numbers in Sakaiminato spiked in 2018 when the sixth television anime series based on Kitarō was broadcast (a project that marked the fiftieth anniversary of the first series). Other events are planned for 2022, which is the centenary of Mizuki's birth. Tottori prefecture statistics (Tottori Prefecture 2021) indicate that the Mizuki Shigeru Road is Tottori's single most visited attraction, making Mizuki's works arguably Tottori prefecture's most important tourism resource ahead of the famous Tottori Sand Dunes.

The success of Mizuki's works both as transmedia entertainment and tourism driver has encouraged scholars to investigate more the

DOI: 10.4324/9781003239970-26

original stories behind his yōkai stories. Takoshima Sunao (2018: 189) has described the great influence of NonNonBa, an old woman in Tottori who told a young Mizuki the yōkai tales that sparked his interest. In addition to this childhood interest, the grotesque and violent scenes in his first work *Hakaba Kitarō* (Kitarō of the Graveyard) suggest that Mizuki's wartime experiences also influenced his yōkai works. In other words, what underpins the success of the Mizuki Shigeru Road and other sites associated with Shigeru is not only folklore and childhood stories but also wartime experiences. In this view, Mizuki tried to talk about his youth and the friends he lost during the war and to pass on these experiences to later generations metaphorically via his yōkai stories.

It is important, therefore, to summarize briefly Mizuki's wartime experiences. In 1942, as a 20-year-old he was studying art and design in Osaka when he was drafted into the military (Mizuki 2007: 63–65). In the autumn of 1943 Mizuki entered his home prefecture regiment, the Tottori Regiment, as a bugler. However, he was not good at playing the bugle and was sent to Rabaul on the island of New Britain as a recruit. Rabaul was a site of intense fighting. When Mizuki boarded his transport in 1943, most ships to Rabaul were being sunk by the Allies. In fact, after his ship arrived not a single Japanese ship reached Rabaul safely thereafter (Mizuki 2002: 83–85). After his miraculous journey to Rabaul, he experienced heavy fighting. In April 1944, Mizuki was sent as part of a unit of around a dozen people to Baien, but they were attacked by enemy troops. On sentry duty at a distance from the main group, he was the only survivor (NHK 2010). He later caught malaria and lost his left arm in an air raid. When he returned to Japan in 1946, he was one of only 80 soldiers to make it home from Rabaul (Mizuki 2007: 98–110; Mizuki 2011: 368).

After the war, Mizuki returned to his youthful interest in art. For years he struggled in poverty as a *kami shibai* ('paper theatre') storyteller and manga artist before his big break came at the age of 43 with *Gegege no Kitarō* (Adachi 2010). Kitarō is the last surviving child of the ghost tribe (*yūreizoku*) and emerged from a grave that represents the world of the dead. This mirrors reality. Mizuki was the last surviving member of his unit, he lost his arm in an enemy attack, and returned home to Japan from the battlefield of death. As Suzuki Shige has argued, 'It is not difficult to see a reflection of Mizuki himself (who had lost one arm in the war) in the figuration of one-eyed, marginalized Kitarō' (Suzuki 2019: 2210). In an interview, Mizuki gave his reasons for creating the character of Kitarō as follows:

> The real reason that I wrote Kitarō is that when I was writing it I was searching for something like a *yorishiro* [in Shinto belief, a physical

object which gives *kami*, "spirits", a place to exist] for my soul. For that reason I did Kitarō. He was a place where my soul could exist.

(Hirabayashi 2007: 26)

Reflecting on his war experiences, he also wrote that 'war turns people into devils' (Mizuki 2010: 51). In this context of Mizuki's treatment of humans during war as devils, 'yōkai are a manifestation of the desires of ordinary people' (Mizuki 2016: 153). Via both clues gained from reading his works and also Mizuki's own words in postwar interviews, it can be concluded, therefore, that his yōkai manga were a significant means via which Mizuki attempted to work through and come to terms with his wartime experiences, particularly as the sole survivor of the fateful mission to Baien.

Mizuki as a manga artist left two main bodies of work: his fictional yōkai manga and non-fictional historical manga, including a manga history of the Showa era and his wartime recollections (the most famous of which is *Onwards Towards Our Noble Deaths*). The connections are evident on a visual level in the similarities between Mizuki's yōkai manga and his war manga. One arresting commonality, noted by Mizuki biographer Adachi Noriyuki (2010), is the loss of an eye (Figure 21.1). The eyeball motif extends to Mizuki's famous character, Kitarō, who loses his eye after being thrown as a baby at a gravestone by a human.

On the level of imagery, metaphor, and content, therefore, the worlds of yōkai and war can be connected as follows. Mizuki's early childhood interests in yōkai and art were interrupted by the war, but when he started drawing yōkai professionally after the war it was a means of expressing what he wanted to say about war. Through careful reading, therefore, his yōkai manga offers insights into his war experiences. In short, Mizuki Shigeru's yōkai world echoes the themes raised in many of the works of culture described by Igarashi Yoshikuni in *Bodies of Memory*. Igarashi's book is 'an attempt to read the absent presence of the country's war memories' (Igarashi 2000: 3) in a range of popular cultural production from art to Godzilla films (see also Chapter 22) to professional wrestling. During the first few decades after the war (Igarashi's study covers the years 1945–1970) the lingering presence of war memories and discourses could be read into much popular culture that, on the surface, was not about the war at all. In the story of Godzilla was the 'absent presence' of nuclear issues; in professional wrestling bouts between American and Japanese wrestlers (especially Korean–Japanese wrestler Rikidōzan) there were subtexts of recovering national pride lost during the war through victory in wrestling. Similarly, the 'absent presence' of war memories is evident in Mizuki's yōkai manga – from the common grotesque imagery,

Figure 21.1 Private Maruyama dies in *Onwards Towards Our Noble Deaths*. Source: Mizuki (2018: 462). ©水木プロ.

the liminal space occupied by the protagonists between life and death, and even the characteristics (whether physical or psychological) between Mizuki and his creation Kitarō. If Mizuki's manga is understood in this way, then all contents tourism relating to Mizuki likewise exhibits the absent presence of war memories and therefore constitutes an important example within the range of activities that may be categorized as war-related contents tourism.

References

Adachi, N., 2010. 'Kitarō' to 'sensō' wo tsunagu mono. *Wedge Infinity*, 18 December. https://wedge.ismedia.jp/articles/-/5737.

Chōfu-shi Kankō Kyōkai, 2017. *Mizuki Shigeru san to Chōfu-shi*. Chofu City Sightseeing Association. https://csa.gr.jp/contents/1701.

Hirabayashi, S., 2007. *Mizuki Shigeru to Kitarō hensenshi*. Tokyo: Yanoman.

Igarashi, Y., 2000. *Bodies of memory: narratives of war in postwar Japanese culture, 1945– 1970*. Princeton: Princeton University Press.

Masubuchi, T., 2010. *Monogatari wo tabi suru hitobito: kontentsu tsūrizumu to wa nani ka*. Tokyo: Sairyūsha.

Mizuki, S., 2002. *Honma ni ore wa aho yarō ka*. Tokyo: Shinchosha.

Mizuki, S., 2007. *Mizuki-san no kōfukuron*. Tokyo: Kadokawa Shoten.

Mizuki, S., 2010. *Haisōki*. Tokyo: Kodansha.

Mizuki, S. (trans. Jocelyn Allen), 2011. *Onward towards our noble deaths*. Montreal: Drawn & Quarterly.

Mizuki, S., 2016. Aratana kōfukugaku wo kangaeru. *In*: Kawade Shobō Shinsha Henshūbu, ed. *Mizuki Shigeru: yōkai, sensō, soshite ningen*. Tokyo: Kawade Shobō Shinsha, 153–155.

Mizuki, S., 2018. *Mizuki Shigeru manga daizenshū 67. Sōin gyokusai seyo*. Tokyo: Kodansha.

Mizuki Shigeru Museum, n.d. *Mizuki Shigeru Road*. Mizuki Shigeru Museum. http://mizuki.sakaiminato.net/road/.

Myoki, S., 2020. Yōkai tourism in Japan and Taiwan. *In*: T. Yamamura and P. Seaton, eds. *Contents tourism and pop culture fandom*. Bristol: Channel View Publications, 98–115.

NHK, 2010. *Sensō shōgen ākaibuzu: Mizuki Shigeru*. NHK Testimony Archive. https://www2.nhk.or.jp/archives/shogenarchives/shogen/movie.cgi?das_id =D0001130006_00000.

Scherer, E. and Thelen, T., 2020. On countryside roads to national identity: Japanese morning drama series (*asadora*) and contents tourism. *Japan Forum*, 32 (1), 6–29.

Suzuki, S., 2019. Yōkai monsters at large: Mizuki Shigeru's manga, transmedia practices, and (lack of) cultural politics. *International Journal of Communication*, 13, 2199–2215.

Takoshima, S., 2018. Mizuki Shigeru sakuhin ni miru minkan denshō no riyō to junshoku. *Ningen bunka: Aichi gakuin daigaku ningen bunka kenkyūjo kiyō*, 33, 164–194.

Tottori Prefecture, 2021. *Shuyō kankō shisetsu irekomi kyakusū*. Tottori Prefecture. https://www.pref.tottori.lg.jp/secure/226511/kankouchi202012.pdf.

Yamamura, T., 2011. *Anime, manga de chiiki shinkō: machi no fan wo umu kontentsu tsūrizumu kaihatsuhō*. Tokyo: Tōkyō Hōrei Shuppan.

22 *Shin Godzilla*

Tourism consuming images of JSDF, *kaiju* characters, and destroyed sites

Aleksandra Jaworowicz-Zimny and
Takayoshi Yamamura

Godzilla, a giant lizard-like monster surfacing from the sea, has been a star of Toho Co., Ltd's movies since 1954, when the original *Godzilla* (dir. Honda Ishirō) premiered in Japan. Since its first appearance, Godzilla was more than just a *kaiju* (giant monster) providing entertainment to cinemagoers. The story of a monster created by a nuclear bomb evoked a number of interpretations as an anti-war message, a portrayal of the Japanese-American relationship, a symbol of post-war moral decline, and most commonly a living symbol of a nuclear bomb (Kalat 2017).

As of August 2021, only within Japan Godzilla has starred in 29 live-action movies (special effects films), three animation films, and one animated television series. The most recent live-action movie, *Shin Godzilla* (2016, dir. Anno Hideaki and Higuchi Shinji) not only brought back the franchise after a 12-year hiatus, but also offered a complete reboot to the series: it is the first movie that does not continue the story after the 1954 original but uses the premise that Godzilla appears for the first time in 2016 Tokyo. Japan is presented realistically, including its landscape, international relations, military equipment, and legal regulations.

In the film, the heroic representation of JSDF (Japan Self-Defense Force) stands in contrast to the critical portrayal of Japan's political leadership. 'The victory in *Shin Godzilla* is a victory achieved through the hard work and sacrifice of Japanese soldiers' (Hall 2017: 156) – they are committed, brave, and ready to die for their country. *Shin Godzilla* pays tribute to JSDF members' bravery in the face of a threat, suggesting a need for strong leadership and effective national defence. Godzilla's attack and the paralysis of the country's political leadership reflect post-2011 Fukushima nuclear disaster Japan, tapping into 'renewed nuclear fears … and the government's subsequent failure to act quickly to ameliorate damage' (Rhoads and McCorkle 2018: 178).

DOI: 10.4324/9781003239970-27

JSDF was not only consulted by the film's producers regarding military language and procedures but also provided equipment and soldiers to appear on screen. Such extensive collaboration would not be possible without a positive portrayal of JSDF in the film (Hall 2017: 151). The production team's records indicate that various steps were taken to secure the cooperation of JSDF in filming: 'the director Anno himself first went to the Ministry of Defense to interview them in order to improve the accuracy of the script' (Toho 2016: 28–30). In addition, the Public Affairs Office at the Ministry of Defense confirmed just before the release of the film that '*Shin Godzilla* is a typical example of the cooperation of the Ministry of Defense and JSDF in the production of films' (interview conducted by Yamamura Takayoshi, 20 July 2016).

Godzilla-related attractions around Tokyo

The film may be rooted in present-day Japanese political issues, but it is also a successful blockbuster aiming to entertain. Toho used the movie's premiere to promote not only *Shin Godzilla*, but the whole franchise. As a result of the studio's strategy and cooperation with other parties, Tokyo, as Toho's home and the location of the movie, gained several Godzilla-related tourist attractions.

Probably the best-known landmark is located in the Kabukichō district of Shinjuku Ward. A fire-breathing 12-metres-tall head of the giant monster was placed on top of Shinjuku Toho Building on 17 April 2015. The statue was planned as part of the *Shin Godzilla* promotional campaign, as well as a new symbol of the ward (Toho 2015). Godzilla was given the title of Shinjuku Tourism Ambassador (*Shinjuku kankō tokushi*) during a special ceremony on 9 April and also received a special ward residency certificate from Shinjuku Ward mayor Yoshizumi Ken'ichi. He expressed hope that the new Godzilla landmark would bring 'new crowds and energy' to the area (ibid.). Hopes for new visitors in Shinjuku, especially *kaiju* fans, rested not only on the Godzilla head statue but also on other attractions. Shortly after the landmark's unveiling, a Godzilla-themed room opened in Hotel Gracery Shinjuku, which offers a close-up view of the landmark. Furthermore, the Godzilla Store Tokyo operated by Toho opened in October 2017. It is a place to get various Godzilla goods but is also an attraction in its own right. It has a human-sized Godzilla figure next to which tourists can have their photos taken. Another statue can be found outside Shinjuku, at Hibiya Square in Yūrakuchō between the Toho office and a shopping mall. Godzilla has occupied this spot since 1995, but in 2018 changed its form to the creature in Anno and Higuchi's film. All these spots are easy to find and access, and are located in areas popular among general Tokyo tourists.

The other type of Godzilla-related attraction scattered around Tokyo is 'sacred sites', or *Shin Godzilla* locations. The Internet has many articles and blog entries providing information about locations, like Tokyo Bay Aqua-Line (where Godzilla surfaced in the film), the Kamata district, Japan Ground Self-Defense Force (JGSDF) Camp Kisarazu, Tamagawa Sengen Shrine, and Tokyo Station. Fans encourage others to visit listed locations by including Google map links and useful information (opening hours, possible fees etc.) in their posts (Shōgo 2020). Pilgrimages can also be supported by local authorities – in Kamata, Ota City Tourist Information Centre produced an unofficial map showing the monster's route (Togech 2016). Finally, some locations offer more than only a view known from the movie. For example, at the Tokyo Bay Aqua-Line fans will find giant Godzilla footsteps in the parking area as a result of an East Nippon Expressway Company initiative (East Nippon Expressway Company Limited 2016).

Contents tourists at JSDF sites

Shin Godzilla has also increased interest in JSDF and triggered contents tourism at JSDF bases. For example, *Seichi junrei hōkoku-sho: Shin Godzilla* (*Shin Godzilla* pilgrimage report), a self-published booklet (*dōjinshi*), contains both movie locations and photographs of JSDF figures during firepower demonstrations (Bōsō Ryodan C Shōtai 2016). It contains information about the military equipment used in the movie and JGSDF Camp Kisarazu. Moreover, *Yasutabi*, a travel information site for women, introduced the annual air festival at JGSDF Camp Kisarazu as one of the recommended sites for *Shin Godzilla*, saying, 'At the air festival, you can actually see helicopters that appeared in the film, and can even board them. This is the perfect event for fans to experience the atmosphere of the film' (Shōgo 2020). For these fans, JSDF is as much a part of the film as Godzilla itself. These are examples of fan initiatives derived from the film's portrayal of the military. The film portrays the activities of JSDF in a more positive light than any previous works, and the weapons are described in a detailed manner. This has led to a high level of interest in JSDF among some fans.

Furthermore, Godzilla has traditionally been associated with tourism, and in particular the enjoyment of finding and visiting places that were destroyed by Godzilla in the films. There is a detailed list of such sites on online travel information site Wikitravel (2019). This kind of tourism is also found in the case of *Shin Godzilla*. In 2018, Ota City and Kawasaki

Figure 22.1 Viewing the place where Godzilla first appeared in *Shin Godzilla*. 'The tower of wind' of the Tokyo Bay Aqua-Line as seen from Umihotaru parking area. Photo: Yamamura Takayoshi.

City collaborated to organize the '*Shin Godzilla* Bus Tour' and the tour's slogan was 'We will visit locations, such as the street where the second form [of Godzilla] was destroyed' (Ota city 2018).

Conclusion

Godzilla-inspired tourism seems primarily character-, weapon-, and destroyed sites-driven, rather than driven by other issues presented in the film. In other words, despite the fact that *Shin Godzilla*, like the first *Godzilla*, can be interpreted as being anti-nuclear, the associated contents tourism is mainly about enjoying the character of Godzilla, seeing the JSDF equipment that appears in the film, and imagining places being destroyed by Godzilla. It induces little tourism that considers anti-nuclear issues in depth.

This is an important issue in terms of how the audience interprets the narrative world and constructs the tourism imaginary. In particular, it contrasts with the audience reaction to *Grave of the Fireflies* in Chapter 17.

Grave of the Fireflies and *Shin Godzilla* contain anti-war and anti-nuclear elements, respectively, but the former induces contents tourism mainly with anti-war intentions, and the latter induces mainly tourism to consume characters, weapons, and images of destroyed sites.

References

Bōsō Ryodan C Shōtai, 2016. *Seichi junrei hōkoku-sho: Shin Gojira.* Bōsō Ryodan, Vol. 13 (self-published *dōjinshi*/fanzine).

East Nippon Expressway Company Limited, 2016. *7.29[FRI] opening memorial 'Shin Godzilla x Umihotaru Campaign' will be held: Shin Godzilla has arrived in Umihotaru!* East Nippon Expressway Company Limited. https://www.e-nexco.co.jp/en/pressroom/kanto/2016/0620/00008192.html.

Hall, J.J., 2017. Japan's anti-kaiju fighting force: normalizing Japan's Self-Defense Forces through postwar monster films. In: C.D.G. Mustachio and J. Barr, eds. *Giant creatures in our world: essays on kaiju and American popular culture.* Jefferson: McFarland & Company, 138–160.

Kalat, D., 2017. *A critical history and filmography of Toho's Godzilla series.* 2nd ed. Jefferson: McFarland and Company [ebook].

Ota City, 2018. *Dai-2 keitai ga hakai shita ano tōri nadono roke-chi wo megurimasu! Ota-ku, Kawasaki-shi renkei jigyō 'Eiga Shin Gojira bus tour' wo jisshi.* Ota City. https://www.city.ota.tokyo.jp/kuseijoho/press/release29/2018022101.html.

Rhoads, S. and McCorkle, B., 2018. *Japan's green monster: environmental commentary in kaiju cinema.* Jefferson: McFarland & Company.

Shōgo, 2020. *[Fan hikken!] Shin Gojira no rokechi to kankō jōho o shōkai shimasu.* Yasutabi. https://yasutabi.info/archives/38561.

Toho, 2015. *Shinjuku Kabukichō ni aratana randomāku ga tanjō! Shinjuku Tōhō biru gurando ōpun ni sakigakete Gojira ga nemuri kara mezameru.* Toho Co. Ltd. https://www.toho.co.jp/movie/news/1504/06godzilla_ib.html.

Togech, 2016. Shin Gojira no seichi junrei ni! 'Kamata-kun' no shinko rūto map ga Keikyu Kamata ekimae ni tōjōchū. *Togech,* 31 August. https://ch.togetter.com/2016/08/31/38998.

Toho, 2016. *Shin Godzilla* (movie booklet). Tokyo: Toho Co., Ltd.

Wikitravel, 2019. Gojira ni hakai sareta yūmei supotto. *Wikitravel: the free travel guide,* 7 October. https://wikitravel.org/ja/ゴジラに破壊された有名スポット.

23 Fantasy wars and their real-life inspirations

Tourism and international conflicts caused by *Attack on Titan*

Ryo Koarai and Takayoshi Yamamura

'Contents' has been defined as 'the combination of the creative elements' (Seaton *et al.* 2017: 2). In this sense, all contents can be called fiction. There is a wide range of war-related contents, ranging from those which strongly reflect historical facts to those which are complete fantasy. Well-known examples of fantasy wars produced by the Japanese contents industry include *Mobile Suit Gundam* (TV animation series, 1979), *The Legend of the Galactic Heroes* (science-fiction novel, 1982–1989), and *Attack on Titan* (manga, 2009–2021). Fujitsu (2021) presents a useful classification schema for animation contents measuring the distance of the contents from historical fact according to whether the story is 'historical' or 'non-historical', or 'linked' to an actual historical war or 'not linked' to one (Fujitsu 2021: 7–8, 120–121). Using this schema, a fantasy war can be defined as a war created at a considerable factual and relational distance from the actual wars of history.

Fantasy wars are consumed as events in a fictional world, rather than as events in the real world, even though fantasy wars may include in some creative way real historical elements in the motifs, characters, and weapons in the story. *Clouds Above the Hill* (Chapter 12) and *Grave of the Fireflies* (Chapter 17) are war-related contents based on historical events which occurred in the real world. By contrast, *Mobile Suit Gundam*, *The Legend of the Galactic Heroes*, and *Attack on Titan* are also war-related contents, but they are not based on historical events and depict non-historical fantasy wars. This chapter focuses on the tourism imaginaries of *Attack on Titan* (manga 2009–2021; TV animation series 2013, 2017, 2018, 2019, 2020–2021, 2022; live-action film 2015) and how interpretations vary internationally.

War in *Attack on Titan* and related contents tourism

Attack on Titan was originally a dark action fantasy manga by Isayama Hajime. The first half of the story appears to be about the battles between

DOI: 10.4324/9781003239970-28

humans and titans. However, in the later stages it turns into a story about war between ethnic groups. The titans, depicted as the enemy of mankind, are an ethnic group called Eldians who are being persecuted and used by another ethnic group, the Marleyans. The story, therefore, is not about battles between mankind and titans, but about war between human beings.

Attack on Titan includes many war-related scenes, such as invasions of other countries by Marley (the nation that controls the titans' power), racism against Eldians, and the actions of various political cabals. All the war-related scenes in *Attack on Titan* are non-historical fantasy events, and Eldians, Marleyans, and all nations and ethnic groups in the story are fictional. As such, *Attack on Titan* has an important characteristic of fantasy-war contents tourism: its story allows audiences in different countries to read messages from the story into the real social issues around them.

Attack on Titan is set in a fantasy world and uses fictional locations. However, it induces tourism in the real world. Nördlingen in Germany is often considered by fans to be one of the model locations for the story because of the similarity of the landscapes (Tabizine 2018). Fans use their imagination to connect Nördlingen's landscape and the fictional city surrounded by giant walls in *Attack on Titan*, and relive the narrative world there as tourists. This type of tourism destination is not a location or a model for a scene but is visited by fans simply because of its similarity to the scenery in the story.

Attack on Titan also generates international tourism. The Japanese TV programme *Why did you come to Japan?* (broadcast 23 August 2019) introduced tourists who visited Japan to see the *Attack on Titan Final Exhibition*, which they visited multiple times during their stay (TV Osaka 2019). In addition, for several years from 2013, when the TV anime was broadcast, the authors observed an international boom among cosplayers to cosplay the characters of *Attack on Titan* at pop culture events both inside and outside of Japan (Figure 23.1).

Attack on Titan also encourages creators' tourism imaginations. It was adapted into a live-action film in 2015, and the shooting location was Hashima Island in Nagasaki prefecture, also known as Gunkanjima (Battleship Island). Nagasaki Prefecture Convention and Tourism Association, which helped with the filming, said the island was selected as a shooting location probably because 'the island's decrepit architectural landscape was close to the image of the blighted city attacked by titans' (Huffington Post 2014). On 11 and 13 May 2014, the staff and cast visited the island to shoot the film (Eiga.com 2015). The original manga, therefore, induced 'creators' tourism' as they searched for appropriate filming locations (Yamamura 2020: 62). Furthermore, as part of Nagasaki

Figure 23.1 A scene from *Attack on Titan* re-enacted by French and Korean cosplayers at Japan Expo 2013. They had both travelled to Paris to cosplay. Photo: Yamamura Takayoshi.

Prefecture's official tourism promotion, Nagasaki Prefecture Convention and Tourism Association and Nagasaki Prefecture introduced a recommended route for visiting shooting locations on their official website (Nagasaki Prefecture Convention and Tourism Association n.d.). This is a typical example of film-location tourism in the manner of other non-historical fantasy-war contents such as *Star Wars, Game of Thrones*, and *Lord of the Rings* (Bolan and Kearney 2017).

Audience literacy, tourism imaginaries, and national conflict

Attack on Titan not only induces tourism but also generates confrontation among fans regarding social issues in the real world. *Attack on Titan* depicts anti-Eldian racism by Marleyans as a problem between two ethnic groups. The story is fictional, but some people read it as a metaphor and interpret the story as having an 'anti-Korean, nationalist, pro-Japan subtext, parallels to anti-Semitic conspiracy theories, and subtextual references to Nazi Germany' (Speelman 2019). But Speelman also notes, 'no one can clearly say what [the author of *Attack on Titan*] Isayama's true intentions are except for him'.

As seen regarding *Grave of the Fireflies* (Chapter 17), gaps can exist between the creators' intentions and audience interpretation, which 'raise various sensitive issues related to historical awareness and political ideas'. In a way, the international issues regarding *Attack on Titan* are even more sensitive. This is not so much a question of creators' intentions, but rather of audience literacy and what messages the audience reads from the content. While *Grave of the Fireflies* is a classic example of the contents depicting historical war, *Attack on Titan* is a typical case of non-historical war. However, both exhibit a gap between the creators' intentions and audience interpretation, and both create imaginaries of real-world problems such as war and racism.

In 2010, Isayama said in his blog that one of *Attack on Titan*'s characters is based on Akiyama Yoshifuru (1859–1930), a general in the Imperial Japanese Army (see Chapter 12). Following this revelation, people claiming to be Korean wrote comments criticizing Isayama's use of Akiyama as a model and his unacceptable historical consciousness (Isayama 2010). Some Koreans see Yoshifuru as a war criminal who 'was responsible for countless atrocities against Korea and China during Japanese occupations' (Speelman 2019). This reaction triggered conflict among fans of different nationalities in East Asia, who have different perceptions of war history. This conflict attracted attention outside of Asia, too (Ashcraft 2013; Speelman 2019). Through transnational consumption, the fantasy-war contents gave audiences in each country the opportunity to make connections between the real world and fictional world, and metaphors allowed the audiences to link real social issues and a fictional story. This process can sometimes generate negative emotions and trigger serious political conflict among fans.

While there are conflicts over historical perceptions among these different audiences, it has not spilled over in any obvious way into *Attack on Titan* contents tourism. The contents tourism phenomena can be seen as a form of entertainment, such as travelling to see similar landscapes to the city in the film, visiting filming locations, enjoying related exhibitions, and attending cosplay events, all of which are separate from the historical issues mentioned in this chapter. In other words, audiences can separate enjoyment of the narrative world of *Attack on Titan* from the war-related issues they can read from the contents. A similar conclusion was drawn regarding *Shin Godzilla* in Chapter 22. As has been demonstrated, fantasy wars induce contents tourism and simultaneously make audiences interested in social issues related to historical wars. Fantasy wars, therefore, are an important category of war-related contents tourism about which much further research is possible.

References

Ashcraft, B., 2013. A thousand death threats against a popular anime creator. *Kotaku*, 1 July. https://kotaku.com/a-thousand-death-threats-against-a-popular-anime-creato-631792221.

Bolan, P. and Kearney, M., 2017. Exploring film tourism potential in Ireland: from Game of Thrones to Star Wars. *Journal of Tourism & Development*, 1 (27/28), 2149–2156.

Eiga.com, 2015. *Miura Haruma, Mizuhara Kiko ra Gunkanjima ni shingeki! Satsuei irai no gaisen ni kanmuryō*. Eiga.com. https://eiga.com/news/20150703/2/.

Fujitsu, R., 2021. *Anime to sensō*. Tokyo: Nihon hyōronsha.

Huffington Post, 2014. Shingeki no kyojin gunkanjima de jissha satsuei. *Huffington Post*, 8 April. https://www.huffingtonpost.jp/2014/04/08/giant-gunkanjima_n_5114867.html.

Isayama, H., 2010. *Kōshin ga todokōtte suimasen! Henji shimasu!* Livedoor blog. http://blog.livedoor.jp/isayamahazime/archives/3639547.html.

Nagasaki Prefecture Convention and Tourism Association, n.d. *Eiga 'Shingeki no kyojin Attack on titan' zenpen/kōhen*. Nagasaki tabi net. https://www.nagasaki-tabinet.com/houjin/report/attackontitan

Seaton, P., Yamamura, T., Sugawa-Shimada, A., and Jang, K., 2017. *Contents tourism in Japan: pilgrimages to 'sacred sites' of popular culture*. New York: Cambria Press.

Speelman, T., 2019. The fascist subtext of Attack on Titan can't go overlooked: the story's twist exposes the ugly side of the manga and anime. *Polygon*, 18 June. https://www.polygon.com/2019/6/18/18683609/attack-on-titan-fascist-nationalist-isayama-hajime-manga-anime.

Tabizine, 2018. Marude fantasy no sekai, bōkenshin wo kusuguru yōroppa no jōsaitoshi 6 sen. *Get News*, 11 July. https://getnews.jp/archives/2060111.

TV Osaka, 2019. *You ha nani shini nippon he?* TV Osaka official site. https://www.tv-osaka.co.jp/onair/detail/oaid=1936046/.

Yamamura, T., 2020. Travelling Heidi: international contents tourism induced by Japanese anime. *In*: T. Yamamura and P. Seaton, eds. *Contents tourism and pop culture fandom: transnational tourism experiences*. Bristol: Channel View Publications, 62–81.

Conclusions

Patterns of war-related (contents) tourism

Takayoshi Yamamura and Philip Seaton

In the Preface, Philip Seaton presented two objectives of this book: first, to elucidate the ways in which *a war transitions from being traumatic to entertaining in the public imagination and works of popular culture*; and second, to examine how visitation to war-related sites *changes from being an act of mourning or commemorative pilgrimage into one of devotion or fan pilgrimage*. This concluding chapter answers these two questions based on the evidence in the 22 case studies.

The first issue relates to the degree of freedom with which war can transition into contents for entertainment. This is primarily a factor of the temporal distance between the historical events and the present. In Chapter 1, we hypothesized that the Satsuma Rebellion (1877) is the cut-off point in Japan before which historical events can be used in entertainment generally free of contemporary political controversy. The case studies up to Chapter 10 (Part II) revealed high degrees of freedom in the creation of war-related entertainment contents. However, from Chapter 11 onwards the degree of freedom dropped. As Jang Kyungjae pointed out in Chapter 3, 'direct stakeholders no longer exist' for most cases of historical events prior to the 1870s. He also observed that the rulers of those eras – such as the Yuan dynasty and the shogunate – 'have little bearing on current national politics' (Chapter 3). In other words, in terms of the three imaginaries of war-related tourism (Figure 1.3), the degree of freedom to create war-related contents tends to be higher for historical events where the imaginaries of subjective war experiences are diluted (i.e. where history is not perceived to be linked to contemporary political debate).

The case studies indicate a more complex situation regarding the second question. The transition of tourism practice from being an act of mourning or commemorative pilgrimage into one of devotion or fan pilgrimage is not a unidirectional change. Rather, the way in which the three imaginaries (collective narrative structures) of war-related tourism

DOI: 10.4324/9781003239970-29

relate to a particular site may change the combination of the three imaginaries, and determine the trends of contents tourism practices. The three
imaginaries are of subjective war experience (*subjective imaginaries*), objective war heritage (*objective imaginaries*), and war-related entertainment
(*entertainment imaginaries*). Moreover, at war-related tourism sites, tourism practices can develop based on the three imaginaries with different
interpretations, norms, and standards of authenticity. Put differently, the
members who share each imaginary correspond to an 'interpretive community' that 'execute[s] the same interpretive strategy' (Fish 1980: 14,
170), or to an 'imagined community' (Anderson 1991).

War-related tourism practices can be classified, therefore, according to
the combination of the strengths and weaknesses of the three imaginaries.
Figure 24.1 shows seven main patterns of war-related tourism identified
in this book.

- *Heritage tourism*: This is broadly speaking tourism at historical sites,
  including sites representing war history. In the context of this book,
  the tourists have little prior identification with the war narrative and
  have not been influenced by pop culture entertainment. Tourism is
  induced by a general interest in history. For example, an Egyptian
  tourist looking at air raid exhibits in the Edo Tokyo Museum.
  Common in international sightseeing.
- *Commemorative pilgrimage and/or heritage tourism*: Strong connections
  exist between tourism and personal identity or education. The war
  events cannot be easily entertainmentized due to strong subjective
  imaginaries, although serious artistic and literary representations are

Types of war-related tourism	Imaginaries of ...			Chapters
	... subjective war experience	... objective war heritage	... war-related entertainment	
Heritage tourism	Negligible	Weak or strong	Negligible	-
Commemorative pilgrimage and/or heritage tourism	Strong	Strong	Negligible	-
Heritage and/or contents tourism	Negligible	Strong	Strong	2-10
War-related contents tourism (war as backdrop)	Weak	Weak	Strong	14, 16-17, 19
War-related contents tourism (fantasy/futuristic)	Negligible	Negligible	Strong	20-23
War-related contents tourism (nationalist)	Strong	Strong	Strong	12, 15, 18
War-related contents tourism (multi-voiced, cosmopolitan)	Strong	Strong	Strong	2, 11, 13

Figure 24.1 Seven patterns of war-related (contents) tourism. Prepared by the authors.

possible. Where popular culture has represented the war, it largely follows or respects the narratives of victims and survivors. For example, Japanese schoolchildren visiting A-bomb sites in Hiroshima. Common at sites of (mass) suffering.

These two patterns of tourism are largely unconnected to contents tourism. Consequently, they have not been discussed in this book. Tourists have not engaged popular culture entertainment representations, either because they are from a different culture (the war is the experience of 'others') or because the war cannot be entertainmentized yet. The fundamental difference is in the importance of the subjective imaginary, which is weaker in heritage tourism and stronger in commemorative pilgrimage.

The next three patterns are all forms of war-related contents tourism. What they have in common is the weak connection to subjective imaginaries of actual wars in history (i.e. the depiction of the war in the work does not generate controversy in contemporary society), which is the key to entertainmentization and tourism.

- *Heritage and/or contents tourism*: This is a concept we first identified in Seaton *et al.* (2017: 10). The wars are at safe 'chronological distance' and do not impinge on contemporary politics, so may be easily entertainmentized. Works of entertainment generate fans of war history who further their interest at heritage sites. For example, samurai drama tourism up to 1877. Common among 'history buffs' and 'history girls' (*rekijo*, Chapter 5).
- *War-related contents tourism (war as a backdrop)*: Fans of the work are visiting related sites, but they are attracted by other elements of the narratives/characters and not war per se. The war is a backdrop which allows accentuated emotions or extraordinary plot devices to be included within the story. For example, *Here Comes Miss Modern* (Chapter 14), *In This Corner of the World* (Chapter 16). Commonly triggered by romance and human drama works.
- *War-related contents tourism (fantasy/futuristic)*: War narratives are largely unconnected to actual history, or the connections are metaphorical/allegorical. War may be easily entertainmentized and travelled. For example, *Shin Godzilla* (Chapter 22), *Attack on Titan* (Chapter 23). Common in science fiction, fantasy, and modern JSDF-related works (Yamamura 2019).

These three patterns are where war as entertainment is most easily consumed in works of pop culture and travelled at 'sacred sites'. They are closest to the broader image of contents tourism (Seaton et al. 2017; Yamamura and Seaton 2020).

The final two patterns are where works of entertainment induce contents tourism amidst politicized discourses of war. By existing at the point of the 'mutually shareable narrative world' (Figure 1.3) such works can be powerful inducers of tourism as they bring together interest in the work as a fan, a desire to learn more about (objective) war history, and validation of the individual's sense of self-identity. In Japan, such works typically depict post-1877 wars and come within the scope of the 'history issue' stemming from issues of Japanese colonialism and war, 1869–1945. People's historical consciousness varies according to political and moral orientation, and using Saito Hiro's (2016) categorizations of 'nationalist' and 'cosmopolitan' approaches to the history issue we can observe two main types.

- *War-related contents tourism (nationalist)*: Works of entertainment reinforce subjective and heritage imaginaries, particularly through themes of service, sacrifice, and patriotism. The works are typically heroic tales of military exploits and adventure, whether ultimately victorious or tragic. For example, kamikaze tourism in Kyushu (Chapter 18), military tourism relating to the Russo-Japanese War (Chapter 12). Common at nationalist/patriotic commemorative sites.
- *War-related contents tourism (multi-voiced, cosmopolitan)*: Entertainment works and tourist sites avoid taking a single side, but rather consciously respect multiple subjective imaginaries and identities. Being multi-voiced reflects a cosmopolitan outlook on historical conflicts. For example, *Golden Kamuy* (Chapter 11). Common when tourism and pop culture espouse transnational and transcultural understandings of historical issues, and particularly when popular culture seeks to understand war history from the perspective of the 'other'.

Regarding these last two, as Yamamura Takayoshi noted in Chapter 2, the evidence for contents tourism induced by multi-voiced works is often inconclusive. Such contents tourism may also look like heritage tourism in the above schema because the desire to learn about history from various perspectives is more obvious than the role of pop culture fandom in inducing tourism. By contrast, there is often clear evidence of nationalist war-related contents tourism (Seaton 2019). Polemical works of pop culture can be powerful inducers of tourism among audiences with which the political message resonates clearly. On balance in the Japanese context, the mutually shareable narrative world (where synergy exists between the tourism imaginaries of subjective war experience, objective war heritage, and war-related entertainment) appears to be more prevalent in its nationalist form, although whether this is actually the case or just an impression gained from the controversy that nationalistic contents tourism attracts is a question for future research.

Finally, this book has also revealed some 'unexpected' aspects of war-related contents tourism that do not fit neatly into the broad theoretical framework we have developed. One example is the metaphorical war references in Mizuki Shigeru's yōkai manga (Chapter 21), which adds an element of war-relatedness to a major contents tourism phenomenon that at first glance is nothing to do with war. Then there are the accidental or unintended connections made between an otherwise uncontroversial form of war-related contents tourism that suddenly politicizes the contents tourism. Examples include the visit to Yasukuni Shrine by a voice actress (Chapter 15) and the revelation that a character in *Attack on Titan* was modelled on a real, controversial historical figure (Chapter 23). The framework presented in this book, therefore, is the first step of a longer research process to study how the theory of war-related contents tourism developed initially in a Japanese context can be refined and improved upon when applied to a broader range of case studies from around the globe of 'travelling war as entertainment'.

References

Anderson, B., 1991. *Imagined communities*. London: Verso.

Fish, S., 1980. *Is there a text in this class?* Cambridge: Harvard University Press.

Saito, H., 2016. *The history problem: the politics of war commemoration in east Asia*. Honolulu: University of Hawai'i Press.

Seaton, P., 2019. Kamikaze museums and contents tourism. *Journal of War & Culture Studies*, 12 (1), 67–84.

Seaton, P., Yamamura, T., Sugawa-Shimada, A., and Jang, K., 2017. *Contents tourism in Japan: pilgrimages to 'sacred sites' of popular culture*. New York: Cambria Press.

Yamamura, T., 2019. Cooperation between anime producers and the Japan Self-Defense Force: creating fantasy and/or propaganda? *Journal of War & Culture Studies*, 12 (1), 8–23.

Yamamura, T. and Seaton, P., eds, 2020. *Contents tourism and pop culture fandom: transnational tourist experiences*. Bristol: Channel View Publications.

Index

Note: Page locators in italics refer to figures.

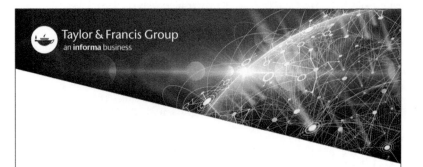

For Product Safety Concerns and Information please contact our EU representative GPSR@taylorandfrancis.com Taylor & Francis Verlag GmbH, Kaufingerstraße 24, 80331 München, Germany

Batch number: 08153772

Printed by Printforce, the Netherlands